I0762968

Praise for

AWAKEN YOUR HIGHEST SELF

"Danny blends raw honesty with actionable wisdom in a way that speaks directly to your potential. His teachings on healing your past, elevating your energy, and returning to your heart are life-changing. Awaken Your Highest Self *will help you create inner peace, purpose, and long-term success from the inside out."*

— **Lewis Howes**, *New York Times* best-selling author of *The Greatness Mindset*

"Awaken Your Highest Self *is the kind of book that doesn't just inspire you while you read it; it challenges the assumptions you live by and gives you a path to rise above them and experience new levels of freedom and fulfillment. Danny has a rare ability to speak to our highest truth in ways that are both undeniable and transformative. If you're ready to stop succumbing to your limitations, this book may be the most effective next step you can take."*

— **Hal Elrod**, best-selling author of 12 books, including *The Miracle Morning*

"This is a beautifully written invitation to rise above fear and reconnect with the truth of who you are. Danny's insights on how our inner energy shapes our happiness are uplifting and actionable. Awaken Your Highest Self *is a powerful companion for anyone seeking emotional freedom, healing, and genuine joy."*

— **Kristen Butler**, founder of The Power of Positivity and best-selling author of *The Comfort Zone*

"I've watched Danny evolve into the powerful, aligned human he is today, and this book captures that transformation beautifully. His message that healing your inner world changes your outer world is exactly what we all need right now. If you want to become a better human—for yourself, your loved ones, and the planet—start with this book. It will open your heart and change your life."

— **Cesar Millan**, creator of the *Better Humans, Better Planet* podcast

"In Awaken Your Highest Self, *Danny Morel opens a door to understanding yourself on a deeper level. His story and guidance show how powerful it can be to listen to your heart and let go of what no longer serves you. If you're seeking clarity, healing, or a fresh start, this book will meet you exactly where you are."*

— **Gabrielle Stone**, best-selling author of *Eat, Pray, #FML*

AWAKEN YOUR HIGHEST SELF

The Limiting Beliefs That Keep You Stuck—
And the Heart Work That Sets You Free

AWAKEN YOUR HIGHEST SELF

DANNY MOREL

HAY HOUSE LLC
Carlsbad, California • New York City
London • Sydney • New Delhi

Published in the United States by:
Hay House LLC, www.hayhouse.com®
P.O. Box 5100, Carlsbad, CA, 92018-5100

Cover design: Pete Garceau • *Interior design:* Karim J. Garcia

Cataloging-in-Publication Data is on file at the Library of Congress

Hardcover ISBN: 978-1-4019-9864-6
E-book ISBN: 978-1-4019-9865-3
Audiobook ISBN: 978-1-4019-9867-7

1st Printing

Printed in the United States of America

This product uses responsibly sourced papers, including recycled materials and materials from other controlled sources.

The authorized representative in the EU for product safety and compliance is Penguin Random House Ireland, Morrison Chambers, 32 Nassau Street, Dublin D02 YH68, Ireland. https://eu-contact.penguin.ie

*For my children, Isaiah, Micah, Aaron, and Selena.
I hope one day you pick up this book and it guides you
as you start the beautiful journey of awakening.
For my wife, Jen, you showed me what it means to Love
and accept Love. I love you all, you are my world!*

CONTENTS

INTRODUCTION

Awaken Your Highest Self

I laid next to her as she took her final breath. My beautiful mother, six years into a battle with lung cancer, was gone. My two brothers and I were with her, yet what I remember the most about that moment was this feeling of not being able to feel. I was in shock. I realized, a moment too late, that I would never again have the chance to hug her, or to tell her I love her, or, our favorite, to dance salsa with her ever again.

She was a devout Christian, and the tough part for me was that she died waiting, praying, and believing Jesus would come and save her. In fact, I was the one who led her to the Lord. She went to church twice a week, tithed, fed the poor on Wednesdays, and waited. I watched her body wither away for years as she kept praying and clinging to her belief the Lord would come and heal her.

He never did, and this made me so mad.

That's when the questions began appearing. *How could a healthy woman get lung cancer, when she had never smoked a day in her life? How could she pass away at such a young age? She was only 61.* So I went searching for the answers. I asked her doctors how it happened. "It just happens," they told me. Then I went to our pastor. "God works in mysterious ways," he said. That line works for most things, and I bought it for a long time, but this was my mom, and something inside of me resisted what the doctors, and the church leaders, especially, were saying.

Everything I was told about life, death, and God no longer made sense to me, and I began questioning even more about God and life.

This was a big deal. I was a deeply religious person, taught to never question, so I never did. I was told to have faith and just believe, so I just did. I was raised Catholic but left the Church and, in my mind, "upgraded" to become an Evangelical in my 20s. When I did, I went all in. I was the guy who went to Bible study and church every week. I knew the book front and back. I memorized the verses. I did everything I was supposed to do. I didn't just go to church—I lived it. I led prayer groups, quoted scripture like it was breath, and believed that faith was the answer to every question. My Bible was worn and underlined. I was all in.

So where was Jesus?

Where was "God" when my mom needed "Him" the most? Why didn't "He" come and save her?

I didn't know it at the time, but I was starting to awaken.

Then I finally got the courage to ask myself three questions I was always afraid of, because deep down, I knew the answers.

Are you happy?

To anyone on the outside, it looked like I had it all, so of course I'd be happy. I had a beautiful wife and three amazing sons. I owned a successful real estate business, employing more than 400 people and doing more than $1 billion in annual sales. I lived in a huge custom-built, Tuscan-inspired home, drove luxury vehicles including my Aston Martin, and wore custom suits and expensive watches. I was on top of the world, and yet all I could think of was, *What is happiness?* I didn't know how to put that feeling into words. I didn't know what it was, because I didn't feel happy, and the truth I was afraid to admit was: I never had.

Do you love what you do, and are you doing what you are meant to?

My life was built around what I did. I got my identity from it. My real estate company was my purpose, and when my mom died, and I looked, like really looked, at my work, I realized, *Oh, my God. I don't think I like what I do.* It didn't light me up. Once I was willing to be honest with myself, I could admit that I wasn't happy in my career. It had me constantly chasing the next deal, the next car, the next house, the next everything.

What I finally started to realize was that I was living in a constant state of fear, fear of the present moment in my work, and that rippled into all areas of my life.

Finally . . . ***are you in love?***

I was 13 years into my marriage, and the sad thing was that I knew the answer to this question the day of my wedding. I was sitting on a balcony, and the videographer pointed a camera in my face and asked, "What do you want to tell your beautiful wife?"

Shit, you better make up something good, I thought.

The sad truth was I had never been in love with my wife. I was in love with the idea of being in love. I loved my sons, and I loved her for having brought them into this world with me, but was I in love with her?

No.

But my religion had taught me to believe that's what you do—you get married and have children. If you didn't wait to have sex till you were married, in the eyes of my religion, you were a "sinner." As a young man, I wanted sex, but I also didn't want to sin, so I believed I had to get married.

I also thought that finding "the one" and saying "I do" would also lead me to happiness, love, and fulfillment. Except I didn't feel love for my wife, and I never had.

There I was, battling with the idea that maybe God and Jesus were not who I believed they were. I was unhappy and stuck in a business that I didn't want to be in (and maybe never had), and I wasn't in love with my wife.

You want to talk about a midlife crisis? I was going nuts. Everything I had built felt like a sham. Looking back, it's no wonder that I was 50 pounds overweight at this time, addicted to food, alcohol, and even porn.

Maybe you've felt this too (or maybe you're feeling something similar now), perhaps not the same vices, maybe not the same weight challenges, but that gnawing sense that the life you've built is missing something essential. That the noise you fill your days with is just a distraction from the silence that feels too scary to sit with. That even the success you've fought so hard to achieve feels hollow.

This is the ache so many of us carry silently until something finally cracks us open.

I wasn't living in my truest, most authentic self, because I didn't know what that was. I had all of these negative emotions, energy, and beliefs buried deep inside that I didn't realize, and as a result, my body was inflamed. I felt exhausted, unfulfilled, disconnected, and miserable, and I couldn't hide from this truth any longer. As I allowed all of the knowledge to penetrate my awareness, and as I began to feel it all, I cried. I mourned. I allowed myself to feel empty and terrified.

Yet, deep in my soul, I also began feeling this lightness, as if a proverbial weight was starting to lift simply because I finally admitted the truth to myself.

And that truth was, I was 43 years old, and I had bypassed myself—my heart and soul—my entire life. I had never stopped to listen to what my heart really wanted. I had never honored myself. Now that I was listening, I realized I wanted more for myself and my life. Not the external trappings I had attained and that had left me empty.

I wanted to *feel* aligned, at peace, and yet also in my power.

I wanted to know what real happiness felt like, to discover my purpose in life and do work that lit me up, to know real love with a woman, and to feel healthy in my mind, body, heart, and soul. Yet simultaneously, I was afraid of the journey it would take to access it all.

Once I stopped hiding from myself, I knew I had a choice. Either I was going to keep living the same life, eventually dying having never honored myself, or this was my moment to step into courage and change my life forever.

I chose courage. And it led me on a spiritual journey that transformed my life in ways that even I couldn't have imagined.

And now, as you read this, I wonder: Where are you in your own life? What crossroads quietly waits beneath your daily routines, your relationships, your inner dialogue? Just like I had to choose, so will you. And when you do, may this book be the mirror that shows you the truth that's been waiting inside you all along.

RETURN TO THE HEART

In the beginning, all I wanted was to discover the truth about myself, life, and to know why I was the way I was. Why had I bypassed myself my entire life? Why was I afraid to say or do what the small voice inside of me always asked of me? I wanted to discover my purpose in this world, to find and know real love, and to learn what I had to do or heal within myself to change my life.

I made a life-changing and sacred decision to go all in on healing and transforming anything and everything that was holding me back from really living. I was willing to let die any part of me that stood in the way. No matter how familiar or comfortable, if it wasn't serving my soul's expansion, it had to go. I set out on a journey across the world practicing and studying ancient healing modalities such as meditation, breathwork, yoga, and plant medicine to discover and heal the invisible, energetic wounds and imprints I carried within me that were unknowingly dictating my patterns in money, relationships, health, and life.

Gradually, and over time, these medicines brought me into the depths of my heart and soul. They became portals that allowed me to confront my greatest fears while unraveling everything blocking me from the inner peace, love, and fulfillment that I was really searching for.

What I found was the very thing that I had spent a lifetime avoiding: opening my heart to receive the energy of love in my life. Not just romantic love. The vibration and frequency of Universal love. The next thing I knew, I was literally Mr. Kumbaya. I felt radiant, connected, and one with Mother Earth, God, and every plant, animal, person, and thing in this world.

As I went deeper into healing and the energy of love, gradually every aspect of my life began changing. I ate healthier and began moving my body more, eventually losing 50 pounds. I moved through a divorce, one of the hardest yet most necessary transitions of my life, and later met and married Jen, my true love. I sold my real estate company, and began a life coaching practice for real estate professionals that slowly evolved into a life and spiritual coaching practice.

I finally felt love and connection in a way I had never experienced before, and I felt so happy on the inside that I couldn't help but want to tell the world about it. I still remembered what it was like to feel miserable, unhappy, and unfulfilled in life. I wanted everyone to know what it felt like to be free, and to know love, happiness, and inner peace. I wanted everyone to no longer feel afraid—of themselves, others, God, or life itself.

I wanted everyone to experience the life transformation that I had, and people seemed to want it too, because they began asking me to teach them how to heal and change their lives. That inner work that started as a personal journey became "Awaken Your Highest Self," a three-day, in-person, immersive experience where I guide people on a transformative journey of self-discovery and healing. Profound healing that takes people on the path of accessing the stories and energy that have blocked them from the life they've always wanted. Blockages that have been in place since they were little children. Many have often said it feels like "30 years of therapy in just three days." Out of the AWAKEN events, my work has evolved into group and private coaching, podcasts, online programs, and deep in-person energetic healing events that we call Intensives.

Even writing this book, I think, *How on earth did the real estate guy become the spiritual guy?* But that, my friend, is the power of returning to your heart and discovering your highest self.

THE JOURNEY AHEAD

What if life isn't as hard, as filled with stress, or as painful as you always thought? What if you *didn't* need to work or try harder, or need more willpower, effort, or motivation to get what you want? What if relationships aren't really *hard* work? What if money *does* grow on trees?

Pause for a moment and reread those questions. Can you make space for that vision? Can you allow room within you for a new reality?

Because if you can, then this moment is the one when everything begins changing.

Most of us have been taught we have to think our way into a better life. But you can't outthink an energetic wound that lives deep in the cells of your body. A wound that no matter how hard you "try" will always find a way to rear its ugly head until you deal with it. You have to become aware of it, feel it, heal it, and then release it at the energetic level. That's the truth, and that's what this book is here for.

When you do this work, your body heals, finances increase with less effort, and you can draw into your life the loving relationships, wealth, and health you've searched for. It's all there for you, and it always has been. Yet to reach this, you have to be willing to unravel everything standing in the way of remembering who and what you've always been. This happens in three stages, which we'll walk through in the pages that follow.

1. Awaken

What are we awakening to? *Everything.*

This is the moment when the veil begins to lift, and you realize that so much of what you've believed about yourself and about life no longer makes sense. Often, awakening isn't gentle. It typically arrives after we face a particularly painful experience where life brings us to our knees—a divorce, loss of a relationship, a serious health diagnosis, being fired or let go at work, or in my case, the death of a loved one. Awakening is the beginning of remembering who you are beyond the labels, boxes, or beliefs or the identity that's been handed to you by others. It's about awakening to your purpose in this lifetime, how and why your life has been created until this point, and the inner heart work you must do to create the life you really want.

2. Heal

The process of awakening is deep because it's truly about becoming aware of what was once hidden or unavailable for you to see, yet the real work comes next: healing. Healing is about going inward to look at surrender and release the parts of us that have been limiting us all along. It's about energetically breaking free of every limitation keeping you from reaching your power, purpose, and potential.

And just past these three, something most humans rarely discover: your calling.

Healing requires us to face what we've been afraid to face and as such will ask us to step into the energy that shifts everything: *courage*.

Remember earlier when I asked you to allow space for a life that wasn't filled with stress? When I offered you the idea that money maybe does grow on trees after all? Those weren't just questions, they were paradigm shifters, each one of them asking you to consider a new frequency, a new way of being. Your willingness to entertain them even for a second was an act of courage, and that courage has already caused a big shift within you.

That's a lot like healing. The only thing that ever stops us from it is the opposite of courage: fear. And so the deeper we go in the book, and the more I invite you to look honestly at your stories and wounds, the more I want you to lean on this truth:

Everything you've ever wanted in life is available to you when you heal.

To do that, you must learn how to release and transmute the trapped energy held tightly within your body, mind, heart, and soul in the form of:

- **Hidden Emotional Wounds:** Painful experiences from your past can quietly shape how you approach love, work, and life, causing repeated disappointments, cycles of pain, and negative patterns.
- **Negative Energy Cords:** Emotional connections to past relationships or difficult experiences drain your energy, leaving you stuck or exhausted without knowing why.
- **Deep-Seated Beliefs:** Ideas from your childhood or family (like "I'm not enough" or "money is hard to get") silently block your path to happiness and success.
- **Energetic Imbalances in Masculine and Feminine Energy:** Childhood or family experiences affect how you express yourself, causing issues in intimacy, confidence, and career.

- **Unconscious Patterns:** Self-sabotaging behaviors (like people pleasing, constantly fighting in relationships, overspending), often formed in childhood, create repeating situations that keep you stuck in your current life and unable to move forward.

3. Transform

When you awaken and heal the trapped energy within, you're ready to alter every aspect of your life, from your health to your relationships, finances, and work. How your life will change is entirely up to you. My intention is to help you become who you've always wanted to be, so you can create a life your heart and soul wants—not the one others have told you to want.

For some, that might be starting a dream business, reaching a career potential, experiencing financial freedom, finding real love, unlocking the deepest level of connection in a relationship, reaching a career high, or experiencing profound inner peace and calm. Really, there is no limit to what you can, or will, create for your life when you heal the energy within and awaken your highest and truest self.

COURAGE AND CERTAINTY BEYOND LOGIC

While I've divided the book into three parts, the journey to awaken your highest self isn't linear. The more you awaken, the more you realize what you have to heal. The more you heal, the more you begin transforming your life. The more you transform your life, the more you begin awakening to other parts of yourself that need healing.

To go on this journey, you need what I call *courage and certainty beyond logic.*

You will face decisions that your heart calls you to make and that will feel right, but won't make sense to your mind. It's not logical or rational. So your mind will scream at you to stop. It'll fight and tell you every reason it can think of why you shouldn't step out of your comfort zone and into the unknown, where you will change your life.

But to reach your highest self, you have to learn to trust something beyond thought.

You must return to your heart—to your feelings, emotions, and intuition—the opposite of rational or logical.

When you're in your heart, you know. When you're in your mind, you believe. Doubt lives in the mind, yet certainty is found in the body. It's going to take courage and certainty beyond logic to learn to trust your heart over the history of your mind.

Anything you want in life is truly possible. I promise you. You're not too late or too broken (you're actually not broken at all). Everything you've been through, every heartbreak, every moment you thought disqualified you, has actually prepared you. It all matters as long as you empower it with your energy. Where you put your focus and energy is what you will see grow, so I invite you to make space for letting go of the negative attachments of the past, to make space for the limitless possibilities of the future.

AWAKEN YOU
Set Your Sacred Intention

I've participated in and led hundreds of retreats, which I treat as sacred ceremonies. Every ceremony begins with setting clear, heart-aligned, sacred intentions to catalyze and crystalize the moment. I invite you to treat this book as a ceremony too, opening it by setting your own sacred intentions.

I want you to go into this ceremony ready and expecting to change a part of your life. When you read the questions below, write the first answer that comes up. Don't think. This doesn't have to be perfect or said a certain way. Just let your answers flow from your heart and intuition; this is how you start connecting, communicating, and listening to your highest self.

1. **What is your intention during the reading of this book?**
2. **What about your life do you want to awaken, heal, and transform?**

The clearer you are with what you want, the more likely you are to receive it. So for example, if I was having a hard time with my finances, my sacred intention might be: "I am ready to let go of and clear any energy blocking me from my truest financial ability," or "I am ready to let go of and clear anything stopping me from financial freedom."

If I keep attracting emotionally unavailable partners, then I might write: "I am ready to clear whatever within me is attracting emotionally unavailable people," or "I am ready to clear any energy that has stopped me from attracting emotionally available people."

If I have a hard time believing in myself, then the intention might be: "I am ready to get to the root of and clear anything that is blocking me from believing and seeing myself."

If I'm having a hard time with my business, then the intention could be: "I am ready to get to the root cause of what is stopping me from seeing my path in my business."

That's it. And if you're unsure what intention to set, that's okay. You could write, "I am ready to discover and heal whatever is holding me back from experiencing more in my life."

Finally, I invite you to close this exercise with the following prayer:

"I promise that I will be an open conduit and channel for love, for remembering who I really am, and for what it is that I am here to seek, discover, and find in this lifetime. I vow to come from love and truth, returning to my heart and my highest self."

PART I

AWAKEN

CHAPTER 1

FROM FEAR TO LOVE

Until my mom died, I was "Mr. Goody Two-Shoes." I was the guy who went to church every Sunday and lived by the book. I never did anything wrong, so much so that when we had a guys' weekend in Cabo, I was the reason wives would let their husbands go. They knew I would keep the guys in line—they trusted me. And I thrived off having created this picture-perfect life as a successful businessman with a beautiful family, surrounded by wealth that had earned me the respect, love, and admiration from others.

And then I blew it all up by having an affair.

I was the last guy you would have expected to cheat on his wife. It was the last thing I ever thought I'd do. I took pride in how straight edge my life was. Yet, looking back, the picture-perfect life I built was really just a beautifully disguised lie. A perfectly and unconsciously orchestrated performance to get me what I yearned for the most: acceptance and admiration. Or as I later learned, what I unconsciously perceived as love.

When the truth came out—as it always does—it destroyed the picture-perfect life I had built. Everything that I clung to unraveled. Truth is, looking back, I can see how my soul orchestrated the entire collapse. It was a perfectly created disaster that drove me to where my ego and need for performance had never allowed me to go—to my knees. I spent most of my life *needing* to be loved, respected, and admired, but now? Hell, people didn't even like me. And strangely enough, that's when everything finally began to change in my life.

When the truth came out about my affair, I did what someone who feels deep guilt and shame often does: I ran back into the known and comfortable. I doubled down and committed to fixing my marriage. I was a people-pleasing good boy who was determined to earn back everyone's trust, respect, and love. The alternative was to get divorced, and based on my religious beliefs, that was untenable. The thought of going to hell and losing God's grace definitely scared the shit out of me. Sure, I had sinned when I had the affair, but I also believed I could atone for that, and God would grant me grace and forgiveness. But a divorce? Absolutely not.

Yet I still knew something wasn't right in my marriage.

I would close my eyes at night and wake up in the morning with the same unsettled feeling. I kept imagining getting divorced, and strangely, every time I pictured it, I felt a wave of freedom and lightness move through me. Still, I was also terrified because I saw myself losing everything in my life if I made that choice. I thought about my kids. I thought about my wife. In reality, I thought about everyone but myself. I was still unconsciously being driven to please everyone, even if it meant continuing to not listen to my heart.

Yet that voice inside of me kept whispering, "What is *your truth*? Do you have the courage to honor it?"

Was I conflicted? You better believe it, but the fear and desire to do "the right thing" outweighed anything else. So I agreed to do whatever it took to make my marriage work, including going to counseling. When you're a devout Christian like my wife and I were at the time, that meant going to the pastor. Our church was massive, one of those megachurches in Southern California. Typically when you need counseling, you get assigned to one of the associate pastors in a church this big. But I was a decent-sized donor and had an established relationship with the senior pastor, so we went straight to the top.

"I feel like the devil is inside of me," I admitted to the pastor as he sat across from me in his office, holding the Bible. "I know the right thing to do is stay in this marriage. I know I did this bad thing having an affair, and I know I'm not supposed to get divorced, yet something in my heart is speaking to me, telling me that it's what's best for both of us. What do I have to heal?"

I felt desperate. I thought there was something very wrong inside of me. I needed the pastor to make it right, and so he did what pastors do. He turned to the Bible and began reading verses to show me why getting a divorce was wrong and a sin.

Except it wasn't working.

I knew the verses. I had them practically memorized, and yet the influence, heck let's just be honest, *the control* they once had over me seemed to slowly be slipping away. I kept waiting for the pastor's words to resonate with me. To move or land with me as *my* truth. I wanted to feel them like I once had, but this time, I felt nothing. It was like the spell had been broken.

When my mom died, something inside of me had opened, and I was becoming more aware of a side of me that had never been online before. The part of us that most men are told to avoid and are even shamed for if we go into. The part of us that women today after thousands of years of disappointment have put a shield around. Her death and the grief I felt had unknowingly triggered the journey of reconnecting with my heart.

The pastor kept flipping from verse to verse, as if he knew he'd find the perfect one. Yet while he was flipping through the pages, I started to realize: Not once had he spoken to my heart. Not once did his words penetrate deep within me or resonate as truth.

It was as if the veil was beginning to lift, and I was able to *see* what I once couldn't. In those words, I no longer saw salvation—I saw fear. I saw the part of me that was afraid to be me—*the real me*—and who thus needed these words, but these verses were slowly slipping away. I saw how the part of me that *needed* someone and something outside of him to lead him was dwindling away in that office. I began to see how I had never allowed myself to listen to and be guided by myself. All I kept thinking was, *What the pastor says makes sense, yet it doesn't.*

I kept hearing over and over the words: *What about your heart?*

It was as if it was a calling, a plea. Something sacred inside of me was finally trying to speak. As the pastor's lips moved and words came out, my inner voice kept asking me, *What about your heart? What about your truth? What about what you feel?*

I was so used to not speaking my truth, so used to pleasing others that I just nodded my head in agreement with what the pastor was saying until finally I felt it. Enough was enough. Finding the courage, I spoke the very words I heard, aloud.

"Pastor, I get what you're saying, but what about my heart?" I said timidly and with some hesitation. "What about my feelings, because to be honest, I feel like I can't love my wife the way she deserves to be loved. And this isn't just about me and what I want. I don't know if I can give her what she needs or truly deserves."

Once I had started talking, the words just poured from me, and I think I must have surprised the pastor because he paused for a long moment before looking me straight in the eyes, unblinking.

"The Bible says the heart is deceiving, Danny."

That was all he said, and then he waited in silence for my response. "I get that," I said, "but what about what I *feel* inside? I don't know if I can keep living like this for much longer." I was practically pleading with him to understand. I wasn't rebelling; I was exhausted from living a lie.

I was ready to be seen. I desperately wanted the pastor to recognize my feelings and to help *me* feel, in my heart, that I was in love with my wife and that staying in our marriage was the right thing for me, her, and our kids. Because I couldn't feel that. If the pastor couldn't change my heart, then I wanted him to at least acknowledge that my feelings mattered and it was okay to listen to my inner self. (I realize now, looking back, that would have gone against everything the Church stood for, as it would challenge the need for its very existence.)

Instead, the pastor leaned toward me and uttered the words that would change my life forever. "Danny, you know all the money you make, your successful real estate business, your beautiful home, your beautiful children, your beautiful wife, and all the love and respect of your fellow parishioners, you know, all of that is God's favor in your life, right?"

I quickly nodded. "Yes, that makes sense. Yes, I know that."

"Well, if you make this decision to divorce your wife, you will lose all of God's favor in your life. You will lose everything important to you—your marriage, your family, your money, your business, your friends and church community—all of that will be gone because God will no longer be with you."

The pastor had voiced all of my greatest fears, yet I heard the small whisper inside again: *Is that love or is that fear?*

BEGINNING IN ONENESS

We are in the middle of creating two separate worlds made of two different energies that both exist on this planet. Each world has different rewards and realities. One world is made up of people living in the *energy of love and oneness*. The other, by people living in the *energy of fear and separation.* Each world carries its own set of rewards, consequences, and experiences. If you're like me, you may not be aware of which one you're living in. Before awakening, I lived in the world of fear, like most people.

But the world of love is also available. To access it, you must first understand that you are more than just a body. You are an infinite soul having a temporary human experience. At your core, you are also energy, constantly vibrating in alignment with the frequencies that live within you. Long before you came into human form—before you had a name or a body—you came from God, the all-knowing, all-loving source of creation. The closest word we have to describe what God is, or the energy of God, is *love.*

A WORD ABOUT "GOD"

God. Source. Creator. Universe. Divine. So which is it? To me it's all the same, all One. When we live in the energy of separation (which we will explore deeply in the book), we separate everything—even God. Yet each word describes the same energy, and the closest word we have to the essence of that energy is *love*. I've gotten to a place in my life where I like using the word *God*, so throughout the pages, you will see this more. But I will also use *Creator, Source,* and *the Divine* interchangeably.

That said, I don't refer to God in the religious sense, or in describing something external. Coming from a Christian background, it's taken me a lot of time and healing to get to a place where I feel comfortable using the word *God* again. After my mom passed, I was angry at God, or actually angry at the version of God the Church gave me. A version that spoke of salvation, if you followed the rules, and spoke of heaven later rather than love now. As I broke away from organized religion, I stopped using the word, replacing it with *Source*, which to me meant the source of all knowing, creation, and love.

This book is an invitation to awaken to your truth. Not a belief system, but a knowing and remembering of the divine light and power that lives within you. So as you read, use the word that feels right for you. If that's *God*, beautiful. If it's substituting *God* with *the Universe, the Divine, the Creator, Source,* or another term that resonates more with you, that's beautiful too.

It's all the same energy, and that energy is love.

Love is not something outside of you, something to earn or achieve. It is the very essence you were made from. Before you arrived here, there was no separation. No "other." The infinite peace, the unconditional love, the abundance—they weren't just around you. They were you.

Love is not something outside of you, something to earn or achieve. It is the very essence you were made from.

When you were in oneness with God, you didn't need to change anything about yourself, to be better or different. You didn't have an identity. Everything was *one*, so there was no better or worse, no past or future. Nothing to compare yourself to or judge yourself against. You were perfect exactly as you were. You didn't regret the past or fear the future, because time didn't exist. You simply were.

So picture this. As a soul, you're up there chilling with God, living in oneness with everything, when you make the decision to incarnate into human form. Not as punishment, but as an opportunity. Why? Because even in your vastness, there are still experiences your soul longs to explore. Lessons to embody. Frequencies to integrate. Earth is literally the school of soul evolution.

And let's be real—life is juicy. Life is wild, unpredictable, and full of flavors that only incarnation can provide. Souls literally line up to be *here*, exactly where you are right now. They yearn to feel, create, cry, laugh, fall in love, lose everything, and rise again. The gift of Earth is that it awakens what was once theoretical into embodied wisdom.

So, you are a soul, and when you were born, you went from the world of oneness to the world of duality—that's here in the physical world. The human experience only works through and with duality, which means two. If you think about it, all of life is duality. For life to exist, there must be one and another. Think of everything that exists, and you'll see the opposite of that thing. A positive and a negative. A beginning and an end. Light and dark. Day and night. The sun and the moon. Masculine and feminine. In a car battery, what must you have? Positive and negative.

And, yes, fear and love.

So you make the choice to come to Earth to work on something your soul has to work on, or to learn or experience, and the next thing you know, you're in your mother's womb. That's where the entire experience begins.

Now, is it light or dark in there?

It's dark. Not the darkness of fear, but the primordial dark—the void, the womb, the beginning. This is the domain of the feminine. Feminine energy, like the mother, holds the unseen, the unspoken, the mystery. It's the realm of the heart, of emotions, of intuition, and of the invisible threads that bind the spiritual world to the physical. It's also the world of transformation and creation, a world you can access and tap into when you're ready to transmute all you've been carrying, release it, and create a new life. Interesting how that sounds a lot like giving birth.

There you are in your mother's womb, growing in safety and comfort, living in oneness and love with her when suddenly her body begins the incredible process of preparing you for birth and literally starts to push you out. It's a beautiful moment, perfectly orchestrated by the Divine, which serves as a transformative portal for both child and mother.

And then in one beautiful moment, you're born and emerge from the darkness of your mother's womb into the light of the physical world. The light represents the masculine—the father. Masculine energy governs the domain of doing, of thought, logic, structure, and the material world. It is linear, directive, and outwardly focused. Where the feminine holds, the masculine builds. Where the mother nurtures the formless, the father brings it into form. From the very beginning, your soul begins the sacred dance between these two polarities—spirit and matter, being and doing, love and law.

Now, imagine what you must have felt when you left the comfort, safety, and bliss of your mother's womb, where everything was provided for you, and you saw the light of the physical world for the first time.

What do you think entered into your awareness?

It was fear. The moment you were born, fear entered your life. Because as soon as you're born, your memories of God, love, and oneness get wiped clean. With your first breath, you were no longer cradled in the womb of unity. You were now an individual, alone, separate, with a name, a body, and a new identity waiting to be formed. You were thrust from the realm of feeling into the realm of thinking. You went from heart and soul to the mind in that instant. From the energy of love, represented by the heart, to the energy of fear, represented by the mind.

The journey you're on, spiritually and energetically, is returning from separation, which occurred at your birth, to the harmony awaiting you when you become one. One with yourself first, then one with God, and finally one with life.

The Journey of Consciousness

The journey I'm talking about is one of consciousness, a gradual expansion of awareness that changes how we perceive, feel, and experience life itself. Most human beings live in what is called the *Third Dimension (3D)*. I'm not talking about Earth. It's not the planet itself. It's not even "reality" in the ultimate sense. It's a field of consciousness—a frequency—or a way of perceiving and experiencing life. For most of us, this is the consciousness we're born into the moment we enter Earth's physical plane. This consciousness is the dimension of separation and survival, of life defined by the external world, by what we can see, measure, touch, achieve, or own.

In the 3D world, we see ourselves as *separate* from everything: from nature, each other, the Divine, even ourselves. We view all of life through judgment and duality—it's either right or wrong, good or bad, success or failure, us or them. In 3D consciousness, time is linear. We live in a constant state of worry about the past and fear the future. And we associate ourselves with our ego identities, believing that who we are and our self-worth is defined by our job, economic class, race, wealth, and appearance.

In this state of awareness, we are unconscious of what's unconscious, and we react to life from past pain, trauma, and programming. In this consciousness, all we are focused on is surviving.

Then there is the *Fourth Dimension (4D)*, known as the bridge or transition between the 3D (physical and ego) and the 5D (heart- and soul-centered consciousness). When we enter 4D, spiritual awakening begins. We become aware that life is about more than our physical reality and ego identities—that a soul-based consciousness exists.

In this state, healing begins. We start confronting past traumas, patterns, and limiting beliefs that have been quietly shaping our lives. We're drawn to practices like meditation, energy healing, plant medicine, and yoga, which help us expand our consciousness and heal. A longing for truth awakens, and we start asking deeper questions: Who am I really? What is life? Why am I here? The inner curiosity begins speaking louder, and we start questioning society, programming, religion, success, and our beliefs.

In 4D consciousness, time also becomes flexible. We notice synchronicities, our intuition sharpens, and manifestation powers begin coming online. Yet, in this state of awareness, we may also start judging the people who "haven't awakened like us," or forming new identities like "the healer" or "the empath," which replace the old ones. This phase tests us. Will we embody love or simply swap one illusion for another?

Finally, there is the *Fifth Dimension (5D)*, the consciousness of love, oneness, and higher wisdom guiding our thoughts and actions. It's a heart-centered and soul-connected way of living on Earth, where we no longer react from fear but respond from love. The Fifth Dimension isn't about escaping life, it's about transforming how we experience it—through presence, compassion, and truth.

In 5D consciousness, separation dissolves. We no longer react to life from fear or ego. We respond with love, alignment, and clarity. Duality fades. There is no judgment, no right or wrong, good or bad, success or failure, us or them. We feel one with everything and everyone and all of life. We flow through life, receiving guidance about our actions from our highest selves, and all of life flows through us as it happens for us.

This is the journey our souls are really on: to transcend 3D consciousness, separation, and survival, and to embody 5D consciousness, grounded in oneness and love, as a human being on Earth. Because we can be physically on Earth but living in a 3D state of consciousness—or in 4D or 5D—depending on our level of awareness, healing, and energetic vibration. Earth holds many dimensions of consciousness, simultaneously. Some people are living in 3D (fear, separation), others are navigating 4D (healing, awakening), and some are anchoring 5D (love, unity, peace)—all on Earth, at the same time.

My intention with this book and all my work is to help you shift from 3D unconscious living to 5D awakened embodiment. It's to walk beside you, aiding and guiding as you move from pain to presence, from ego to soul, from fear to love, and from limitation to truth.

TRAPPED IN AN ILLUSION OF SEPARATION

As I mentioned, most people live in the 3D world built from the energy of separation and survival. What do I mean by survival? It starts at the very beginning. When you were born, you were pure joy, because you had come from love and you only knew love. Now, I want you to pause and think of any child you know between the ages of zero and two. Really picture them and notice how they move through the world. They're expressive. They're happy, smiling, laughing, playing. They love to explore the world and are curious to touch, taste, feel, smell, see, hear all that there is to discover.

This is your original state. This is your essence before the conditioning began, but then you were born into a world shaped by your parents (or caretakers), who raised you based on their beliefs, doubts, fears, worries, and disconnection. And what this meant was that along the way, you learned that to feel safe, powerful, and to get what you wanted, you had to listen to those who seemed to control your life. You were told if you made a "wrong" choice, there would be consequences—maybe you'd be scolded, punished, put in time-out, or even hurt, simply for exploring, expressing, or being your full self. And in that punishment, you started to learn very early, you weren't the creator of your life. Something or someone outside of you was.

Then you went to school, and dealt with a teacher who had their own set of beliefs, dramas, and life circumstances. You didn't know anything about that teacher. You didn't know if they had a great family environment or if they were struggling with mental illness. All you knew was the teacher called the shots. Now you have both your parents and the teacher telling you how to live, how to behave, and what to think.

This gets even deeper, because imagine you grew up in a lower-income household like I did. Those you look up to are probably stressed out, and it means you're going to school in a lower-income district, which usually leads to a stressed-out teacher, because she's not being paid much either. These people control whether you eat, how you eat, and predominantly how you feel.

What you're learning is that life is outside of you versus inside of you.

This lesson keeps getting hammered into you again and again, because then religion enters the picture, reinforcing the belief that God is outside of you. And not only is God outside of you, but in some religions, like Christianity, which was mine, you're taught that Jesus died for you, for something that you and all of humanity did wrong. Now it's a triple whammy. You have a layer of guilt for something that you believe you did, and you keep getting programmed with story after story that teaches you the same thing: Life, love, truth, even God are all outside of you, and you need someone else, some authority, to tell you who you are and how to live.

So first you have your parents or caretakers, then school, religion, now here comes the government. If my parents were awakened people, I would have learned that it didn't matter who the president was, because I'm the creator of my life. But most parents are so used to giving away their power that they give it away in politics too, believing people like presidents have more power than they do to determine the outcome of their life. You're taught to believe this too, so over time, your sovereignty, power, and divinity is stripped from you. And it all happened the moment you were born.

In many indigenous cultures, children are seen as sacred, because they just came from the Creator. In the Lakota tradition, the word for child is *wakaneja*. It comes from two words: *waka*, meaning "sacred," and *yeja*, meaning "gift." In many indigenous traditions, parents and elders leaned in to guiding and nurturing a child's development—physical, emotional, and spiritual—rather than attempting to coerce, control, or mold them a certain way.

But in Western society, it's the opposite. Unconsciously, you become separate from your ability to create, to live, to manifest, to become your full potential and highest self, because you've been taught, since your first breath in this world, that power is not yours. That it lies outside of you, when really, it's always been within you, simply waiting for you to remember that and return to it.

I'll take it a step further, as the influence doesn't stop once you're an adult. After you finish school, and you go into the working world, you might start feeling deep inside that something's not quite right. You may not be able to pinpoint what this is, but you sense it. That's your soul remembering. It knows the truth: that you are one with the Creator. It knows you hold the power to shape your reality, to live freely, fully, and in alignment with your deepest purpose.

Yet somewhere along the way, that truth was buried. That power was stripped from your awareness, replaced by systems that taught you to obey, conform, and stay small.

Society then steps in to teach you that happiness and joy can only be found outside of you. It's in getting married, in how your body looks, in how much you earn, in the clothing brands you wear, the house you live in and zip code, and in your job. So you start chasing and creating this life based on that message. Even when you reach the place where you say, "I want to change my life," and you start on a spiritual journey, you're taught to believe in ideas like "The Law of Attraction," as if even your ability to attract is in a box called a "law."

No. You are attraction. You are the field. You are the magnetism. You are already everything you've ever wanted.

You are attraction. You are the field. You are the magnetism. You are already everything you've ever wanted.

This chapter is here to help you remember that in order to begin the shift from 3D to 4D and, eventually, into 5D consciousness. It's a return, a sacred unlearning of everything that ever separated you from your oneness with yourself, God, life, and your ability to create whatever you want.

Because it comes down to this: You either live in separation or you live in oneness.

What I'm about to share with you will challenge every part of your subconscious belief system. It has to; if not, you'll stay stuck in separation, disconnected from your authentic self, from your heart, and from the truth you've always known deep within.

The Tricks of Separation

What's the first thing that happens after you're born? You're given a name. You're Samantha. I'm Danny. You are one person, and I am another. We're separated immediately, and then we're taught to create an identity for ourselves based on things outside of ourselves. What are those things? Let's break them down.

Race

One of the first and most powerful stories we're handed is the idea of race. Think about it—babies don't come into the world judging each other by skin tone. But very quickly, society begins to assign meaning to color. You learn what it means to be "white" or "Black" or "brown," and with that comes a long, painful history—one that you didn't choose, but that starts shaping your worldview.

Lighter-skinned people are somehow considered more beautiful, more abundant, or more privileged. Darker-skinned people have to work harder, prove more, and endure more.

Pause for a second. What if this is all a lie?

What if all along the energy of separation has tapped into the pain frequency within you, causing you to think that you are separate from other people based on the color of your skin?

Growing up, my favorite American hero was Dr. Martin Luther King Jr., who dreamed that one day we would judge people based on the content of their character, not their skin color. And yet, do we actually do that? Pause for a moment.

Don't think about cops right now, don't think about anyone outside of you. Don't go to where the programming of the news continuously tries to keep you. Stay within yourself, the only place where you have control.

Do you judge people based on the content of their character or the color of their skin? Do you judge yourself based on the content of your character or your skin? Do you look at the inside first or the outside?

I had to ask myself these questions too. My entire life, I was told that I was a minority, that I was less than. I didn't realize it until I started to look inside, but for most of my life, a part of me believed I had to prove that I wasn't less than others.

And that's when I had a thought, which changed how I saw myself and everyone else in the world: Racism can't exist by itself. It can't exist out there if it doesn't exist inside of us first. If I'm walking down the street and people who don't look like me scare me, they haven't done anything to me, it's simply me judging them.

Politics

Politics is built on us versus them. And both sides, at their core, believe the same thing: They're right and the other side is wrong. What's wild is they're both right and wrong. When either side believes the only way forward is through attacking or defeating the other, they lose their own humanity and life force. That's the trap of polarity.

Now, I'm not saying that what happens in our government doesn't matter. It obviously does. What I am saying is once you tap into the Creator within, who gets elected will never have power over your inner peace or the results in your life. You'll realize you have the ability to change your life and to do whatever you're truly called to, no matter what's happening "out there."

Culture/Family

Our culture, or family, keeps us looking at life from the lens of how it lives, not what is necessarily right for us. I was raised with the belief that family comes first, and I should honor them before myself. Don't get me wrong, I value and *love* my family, and I honor the sacrifices they've made for me. Yet as I grew up, I realized my family's beliefs and values didn't always align with mine. The lives we wanted to create were different. Not right or wrong, different.

For example, I was raised in a culture where any time my relatives came to town, it was expected that they would stay at our house so they could save money. We didn't have the space, so people would spread out on the floor, squeezed into every corner. Yes, it created wonderful memories, and yes, I genuinely love supporting my family. Yet I also hated feeling like I had no choice. My energetic makeup craves its own space, but I didn't feel I could say this, and I didn't believe I could set a boundary like this, because I was taught that "family comes first."

What often happens in situations like this is we're taught to bypass our intuition and needs. We learn to put what our family or culture values ahead of what our inner self knows is right or wrong for us.

It's not that our families intentionally are trying to hurt us, or discount our needs, or want us to disconnect from our inner selves. It's simply that they too were once conditioned to put the needs and wants of the family first, accepting the family values as their own.

The last thing most of us want is to be cast out of our tribes. At a very basic level, it's simply about survival. We literally need our parents and families for everything when we're young, and so we grow up accepting the needs and wants of them before our own so we fit in.

But by putting the needs of the family first, we are taught to disconnect from our sense of self, power, and divinity.

Nationality or Country

One of the biggest decisions you'll ever make in life is choosing which self you live from—the societal or the spiritual. The societal self sees itself as separate and identifies with one country and one flag.

When you identify with your country, you automatically separate yourself from people in other countries. And each country carries its own frequency. Some want to be superior, others humble, some to not be seen, and others want to dominate and be in a constant state of war. So when you identify with a country, then that country's energy field begins to influence your own.

For a long time, I identified with being an American. But the deeper I went in my spiritual journey, the more I questioned what that actually meant. There's a lot about the United States I love and dislike. No one ever talks about what we did to the Native Americans, how we murdered, persecuted, stole their land, and lied to them. How we literally rewrote history to feel good about it, and because we've never fully acknowledged or reconciled that energy, it still lives in the collective body of this nation.

Why do you think the US is never at peace within itself? Ever wonder why we're always in some sort of battle or division, constantly debating and fighting with each other? It started with our founding, and until we reckon with that energy, it will continue influencing us all in subtle and unsubtle ways.

I'm not saying don't love your country. Love it. Honor it. Let it be a part of your story but not the whole of who you are.

Where the societal self sees separation, the spiritual self sees only one planet and one people. All of humanity is one. I dreamt of building this beautiful home at the base of a mountain in Southern California, and so I did. That home meant everything to me. I loved the feel of the land. I held several plant medicine ceremonies there, brought friends together, and everyone who stepped foot on that property could feel it was a sacred place. One day, I decided to go on a backpacking trip to Colombia to reconnect with my ancestors, the land, and people, and when I got home to California, my ex-wife told me she was moving to Austin and taking my three boys with her.

Before my trip, I never would have imagined I could leave my California home or the land. Yet in Colombia I was shown how there are no borders or boundaries in this world, there are no countries or nations of people. Humans made them all.

When my ex-wife said she was moving, I said, "Okay. I'll go too." And the only reason I could let go of my dream home in California was because I had started to disconnect from my identity as an American. I was starting to see myself as a human being, and my land was

Earth. My people were all people. And my home was wherever my boys were. Not a country. Not a place. Not a people.

My home was love.

Economic Class

At one point in time, human beings didn't need money. We all lived in community, sharing everything, and helping each other to survive. This is very simplistic, but the basics are old. Some people would hunt, others gathered, others cooked, built shelters, or cared for the sick and wounded, and we raised our children together.

Then came farming and agriculture, followed by bartering, specialization of labor, and then money. Whereas we once relied on our community to live and survive, that responsibility came to fall on the individual and their immediate family. Eventually, human beings' very survival and identity became attached to how much money we make or don't. Do you have money to buy food? Housing? Clothing? Medicine?

And then economic classes were born. Society handed us labels based on income—lower, middle, upper—and we believed them. Each class has its own assumptions, expectations, and energetic cages, all created by us.

Religion

I realize for some people, what I'm about to say might be difficult to read. Many of us, including myself, were raised believing that we can never question our religion, its teachings, or its leaders. First, know that you have done nothing wrong. What I'm about to write is not about you and your beliefs, because you were taught to believe certain truths and teachings. If you're open and curious to hear a different view on religion, then continue reading this section, and if you feel uncertain, then skip to the next one and know that wherever you are is exactly where you need to be. So no judgment if your inner self says to move past this for now.

Now, picture going to the hottest club in town. You have all your friends with you, and you're ready to dance, party, and have a great time. You get to the doorway and suddenly some big, burly guy is standing with his arms crossed, brow furrowed, in front of the door telling you "no one gets in except through me."

This is what happens in organized religion.

Religion reinforces the idea of separation, telling us we must look outside of ourselves and to turn to someone else to reach, hear, or speak to God.

And not only does religion keep us separate from God, it keeps us separate from each other. If I think my God is the one and only real God, then by default whatever you think is wrong, because we both can't be right.

HOW THE ILLUSION OF SEPARATION WOUNDS US

When we're living in separation, society is waiting to offer us its versions of salvation: alcohol and drugs, sex and relationships, careers and success, possessions and power. But the more we chase what's outside, the more disconnected we become from what's inside. We get trapped in an endless cycle of seeking, never realizing that everything we've ever wanted has always lived within.

That's what happened to my friend Pete. He told me that his entire life, he felt "different." As an adult, he stood about five foot four, and as a kid, he was relentlessly bullied for his size. He was also the only dark-skinned kid in his school, constantly picked on for not speaking English—he was originally from Lebanon—and his family was poor. He grew up without a father too.

Basically, he experienced all the tricks of separation at once, and it drove him to want to feel powerful, as most of his life he felt powerless.

When men want to feel powerful, it can show up in different ways. One is with their body. Some men obsess about oversized muscles. This happens when someone is unconsciously led by a desire to protect themselves. Larger muscles can act as an external sign that shows "you can't hurt me."

Sometimes, this can lead men to become addicted to steroids. The needle becomes an external symbol that life, strength, and power can only be found outside of themselves. Without the needle, men believe they cannot be safe. Deep inside, these men are afraid of allowing people to see or get to know their real selves. (Women, too, are subject to the illusion their value comes from the external.)

Pete sought power through having huge muscles (he was addicted to steroids) and possessions. He owned a *ton* of fancy cars—two Lamborghinis, two Ferraris, a Rolls-Royce—plus a multimillion-dollar home. I remember on his wedding day, hundreds of people were there, and when you pulled up, the first thing you saw were his cars parked outside as if lined up on display. It felt like Pete wanted his guests to walk by in awe and say, "Wow, look at how rich Pete is."

This was around the time when I was awakening, so when I looked at Pete, I saw my old self—a person living in a constant state of despair, craving, anxiety, and probably humiliation from his childhood. I saw a man who needed the external validation of his cars to prove he was worthy, and the steroids to bulk up, so he could never be hurt again. I saw beneath it all, and I thought, *Pete is really sad inside his heart.* The muscles and the cars were a distraction.

Pete was only married a few years and got divorced shortly before COVID-19. From the outside looking in, you'd have thought Pete was one of the healthiest people—he had big muscles and worked out constantly. But I knew his emotions weren't healthy.

And when Pete caught COVID, he died. At his funeral, I sat in the pews feeling sad and enraged. His family hired a well-known pastor, and everyone who spoke about Pete talked about his cars and how he wanted more.

*Are you kidding me? His f*cking cars?*

As if Pete's worth could be reduced to metal and wheels. Yes, he wanted more cars, but deep down, I believe what he really wanted—what we all are actually seeking—was inner peace. I think he wanted to experience love, acceptance, and validation, which he never had because he lived, like so many of us, in the energy of separation.

Separation drives us to constantly crave more but to never find it. This energy wants us to believe *we* are not enough. In the energy of separation, we'll always find a way to *be separate.*

Because in this energy, our hearts are broken.

If they weren't, we wouldn't seek answers for how to live our lives, what to believe, or who to be outside of ourselves. We wouldn't feel the need to compare ourselves and lives to others, and as a result, judge people, experiences, things, and ourselves as "right or wrong" or "good or bad." We wouldn't constantly crave more.

We'd just be.

The first step in awakening is understanding how many paradigms you've been conditioned to fit into based on your deep need to belong to something outside of yourself. And if you're unsure, just ask: Is this love or is this fear? When you start looking closely at your life, you'll likely realize how much separation has ruled *everything*—how every thought, belief, story, and even emotion is controlled by it. Once you start waking up to the energy of separation in your life, then you have the power to say "no more" to all the tricks it has played on you.

BY DAWN'S LIGHT

By default, it's like we're asleep, walking around absorbing all of these negative thoughts, feelings, beliefs, and stories from the world and the people around us. Society doesn't want us to come back to love. The media doesn't want us in peace, and, yes, dark energy doesn't want us in oneness, because as long as we live in fear and separation, we can be controlled. That energy wants us stuck. It feeds on our fear, and so its survival depends on it.

But oneness is light. It feeds life and gives more of it to everyone that accesses it. The beauty of it all is the power to choose which energy you live in lies within you.

You're being called to awaken. To become aware of how our world was designed and how you have been trapped, living in the world of fear.

When I started to recognize all the ways we're taught to live in separation, it reminded me of the movie *The Matrix*. There's a scene where the mentor, Morpheus, gives the main character, Neo, a choice. He can take the red pill and learn the truth about reality and the world he's been living in, or he can swallow the blue pill and return to his life having forgotten everything. Neo chose the red pill, and his life was never the same.

This is your *Matrix* moment. Like Neo, you don't need to know what's on the other side of the pill to take it, even if you've already caught a glimpse. I remember my red pill moment, when I sat before the pastor and he told me that I'd lose everything because I'd lose God's favor if I got divorced. All I could think was, *I may not know what love is, but I know it's not that.*

What I felt from him was fear, guilt, and manipulation, and in that moment, I saw two clear paths ahead of me.

Down one road, everything I already knew.

Down the second, a life of uncertainty, of the unknown.

My mind—the logical, rational part of myself—screamed at me, saying the same things as the pastor. *You'll lose your kids, the house, your business, your money, even your church community if you choose to get divorced,* I heard.

Yet my heart and soul knew the truth, and so I made a decision. I would rather live in a cardboard box, broke and jobless, having lost everything, than to stay living in fear one more day. I was willing to die, but I wouldn't live in fear anymore.

From my heart, I chose to live in love.

I got divorced, and the pastor and my logical, rational mind were right. That decision cost me everything. I lost my home and lived in a tiny apartment. I eventually sold my business to another company, yet kept shares. All the cash I received from the deal, I gave to my ex-wife so she and the boys would be safe. I thought I made a great deal. The new business was buying other companies, and I was the largest shareholder. Turns out, the company I sold to was fraudulent. I had given my ex all the cash and real estate and still owed her millions of dollars, and I had nothing coming in. I was single for more than three years. I left the church and lost most of that community and my friends too.

And yet losing it all showed me the pathway to everything that my heart and soul had ever wanted, but that I had been too scared to let myself dream of and create. I wouldn't be where I am today if I had said, "Yes, sir," and went along with the pastor. If I had listened to him, then I'd still be stuck in fear.

Like me, you've been living in the world of fear. Not because you chose it, but because it's what you were born into. And in this world, you were taught to believe you're separate. Now you know the truth. You aren't the identity you've been made to believe you are. You *can* be, but notice how that identity (whatever it is) instantly disconnects you from everyone else.

The truth is, you're more than a nationality, religion, culture, or economic class. You're more than the material possessions you've been taught to strive for.

You are a soul.

A soul on a human journey who is free to create whatever you want. A soul that is tapped into the energy of love and oneness with the Creator, and who is never alone.

When you realize this oneness, then all of the stories, limitations, and beliefs that say you're separate, all the barriers keeping you from everything you want in life, simply disappear. Everything you've been holding on to around your heart—the pain, protection, and proving—it vanishes. In its place lives the ability to call in the life you've always wanted.

It's not just about creating the life you want either, it's about creating *the world* you want to live in. Because as long as the energy of racism, poverty, religion, or any of the tricks of separation live inside of you, they will live in the world. If you want to end racism, poverty, war, any of it, guess where it has to end first? Within you.

When the energy of separation ends within you, it ends in the world.

The deeper you go into your healing, the more you will discover a simple truth: *Something always has to die for what you truly want to live.* The first thing that has to die on this journey is the old paradigm, the belief, heck, the old life that you've been living in separation. It has to go to make space for the new to come in.

If you want racism, poverty, war, and ultimately separation to disappear from the world, guess where it has to end? Within you. When it ends within you, it ends in the world.

Right now, all you have to do is decide. Make the decision in your heart which world you choose to live in. Fear or love. That's it. You don't need to know how it will turn out. You don't need a plan or action steps. All you have to do is choose.

So choose and declare from the stillness of your heart, from this day forward, which world you will live from: fear or love.

AWAKEN YOU

Discover the Tricks of Separation

Sit in stillness for five minutes and scan your life including your relationships, career, money, and health, or return to the tricks of separation and pick one that calls to you. Then ask your highest self (God, the Universe, or the Creator) to show you what is blocking you from living in the fullness of your heart. Ask this question aloud, then once silently with your eyes closed:

"Dear God, is this blocking me from living in the fullness of my heart and highest self?"

Feel your way to the truth. Notice if you get a little ping in your body. Do you hear an immediate yes or no? Do you feel something in your stomach like a hunch? Do you feel hot or cold? Listen for the answers as they come to you through your body and senses. For me, I often hear whispers, or I feel something is for me or not for me in my gut or heart. The more you practice communicating with your highest self, the easier it becomes, so stay open in your mind and heart, and listen.

CHAPTER 2

LOW-FREQUENCY LIVING

About three years after my mother died, my life was turned upside down. I had sold my real estate business, had gotten divorced, and was on a journey of discovering myself. That journey led me to work in a deep manner with plant medicine. I went on back-to-back, week-long ayahuasca retreats dealing with some of the deepest emotions that I had been afraid to deal with in my life.

I faced all of it, and in doing so, I had experiences that helped me realize I wasn't alone in this journey of wanting to heal. I wanted to help people transform their lives in the ways that I was transforming mine, so I started leading small groups to Mexico and other countries in Central America for ayahuasca and other plant medicine journeys.

I was getting ready for our next trip when something felt off with my assistant. It was really strange. She had been with me for three years, and I had never felt *anything* like that before. I couldn't pinpoint it, but something just didn't feel right about her energy, and I heard that small whisper inside of me say, *"She's not allowed to come on the retreat."*

She's not allowed? I thought. *What a strange message.*

"Why isn't she allowed?" I asked the voice.

I didn't get a response, just a strong feeling that she wasn't supposed to have anything to do with the organizing of the retreat. By now, I was listening to and honoring the messages I was receiving, so although it didn't make sense to me, I told her she wouldn't be needed. I didn't think anything of it. We went and had a beautiful journey, and as always, the medicine showed up in a big, miraculous way and changed people's lives.

A couple of weeks later I learned why she wasn't allowed on the trip.

She had been stealing from me.

My assistant, whom I had trusted without question like I do with most everyone, had booked two first-class tickets for her and her husband to Hawaii and paid the rent for their apartment using my credit card. She even stole money from the plant medicine journeys that we were leading people on.

I was stunned. I felt hurt, betrayed, and enraged. In my mind I thought, *How could this have happened to me? Why did she do this to me? Why did God allow this to happen to me? I have been honoring my truth, listening to my heart, yet something like this happens? How dare she steal from me?*

I was pissed at God and life, I was blaming my assistant, and, yes, I'll admit it, I felt like a victim. Then something interesting happened when I sat in meditation.

"Danny, you created this," that inner voice said.

"No, I didn't," I shot back.

"Oh, yes, you did. Look deeper. What was the energy you were in when you hired her? What was the energy you were in that attracted that person?"

*F*ck. . . .* It all came to me, and it felt like it smacked me between the eyes and punched me in the gut at the same time. When I searched within, I realized that when I had hired my assistant, I was in the middle of my affair.

THE WORLD IS YOUR MIRROR

Everything in our world and all of life is made of energy—including you. All of your thoughts, emotions, and every experience that you've ever had is simply energy vibrating at a low or high frequency. And it is this very frequency within you that calls in the very people and experiences in your outside world to match the energy inside.

So think of the world as your mirror, because it is.

The energy within attracts the life without, so you are literally attracting life from the inside out. Everything you have on the outside—the partners you've experienced in your love life, the money you earn or don't, even the current state of your health—all of it is simply a vibrational match for what you think, feel, and believe on the inside.

Imagine a giant projector that lives inside of you, sitting at the center of your chest, and picture a lens that faces and projects out into the world. So based on the energy inside of you, which consists of what you feel, your limiting stories and beliefs, and unhealed wounds and trauma, you project that out into the world and call in the people, circumstances, and experiences that are a vibrational match for what's within.

It's not the Universe. It's literally *you inverse.* Or in other words, *you inside out.*

It's not the Universe. It's literally you inverse. Or in other words, you inside out.

When I hired my assistant, I wasn't being truthful. I was living in a season of dishonesty, deceit, and violating people's trust. So the energy that was most active within me called into my life someone who was an exact energetic mirror to me.

This is literally happening with *everything* in your life. How much money you make, how you make it, your career, the company you lead, the clients you attract, the person you're in relationship with who mistreats you, drives you crazy, or loves you, the health you experience, *all* of it is based on how chaotic you are within, how you talk to yourself, and even the way you love yourself. Everything is a reflection of what's happening inside.

And so much of what you see projected outside is about how you see yourself. The more you love yourself, the more valuable and abundant you feel. The more valuable and abundant you feel, the more you will prioritize yourself. The more you prioritize yourself, the more you will honor yourself. The more you honor yourself, the more you will protect yourself. The more you protect yourself, the more you will only allow the best food into your body, the best partner and friends into your life, and the best clients, co-workers, bosses, and employees into your business or career.

You literally are the creator of it all. You always have been, and you always will be.

Let me show you another example. Mary owns million-dollar businesses with her husband, yet she felt something was missing. "I wasn't stepping into my full power," she said. "I didn't realize it at the time, but the evidence was all around me. My marriage was a train wreck. My children were assholes, and I wasn't happy, even though, as the leader of our organization, I portrayed this positive attitude and told everyone that everything always works out.

"But when I started to get quiet inside and looked at myself, I realized I felt out of control. I had a sense that life was just happening to me, and I had to accept it all—accept that my husband ignored me and we had virtually no physical or romantic relationship, accept that my kids treated me like a doormat, maid, and chauffeur, and accept that my employees didn't have to have accountability or responsibility.

"As soon as I became aware of the fact that *I* was the one creating it all, I went all in on healing the energy within me that was causing it, and that's what changed everything. I started to realize that I'm the one who gets to decide the type of relationships that I will allow in my life, and I'm the one who decides how I will be treated by my husband, my children, and my employees, and this is when everything started shifting for the better."

Why did it shift for Mary? Because she began the journey of shifting the energy inside and raising the vibration in which she was living. She began to become aware of all the ways in which she had allowed people to treat her, ways that were unloving. And at the core of it all was how unloving she was being to herself.

Most of us, like Mary, don't look at what's happening in our lives first, then go inside and take action on it. We get used to what's happening, and we start to blame other people for what's going on, and then we die without ever having seen the real reason for the people, circumstances, and experiences. Everything is trying to point us inward to show us what we have to heal.

Let me give you another example. I often hear people say, "Danny, I want to find my dream partner and soul mate."

That sounds so beautiful, and I always ask this with so much love: Are you serious? Do you know what your dream partner is actually going to do when you call them in? The sole (soul) purpose is to reflect back to you all of your deepest, darkest stuff. A real soul mate causes you to be so uncomfortable that you'll feel like leaving, except you love them, and they love you, so you can't leave. If you allow it, then together, you'll help each other heal the hidden parts of yourselves that not even the greatest books, podcasts, or plant medicine journeys can heal.

Yet, what do we do as human beings? We're so busy fighting and arguing with each other over little shit like the dishes, or the sink not being cleaned, we never stop to ask ourselves this magical question: Why does what they do bother me so much? Maybe the little things that bother me about them are actually here to show me a deeper part of myself that I've never acknowledged, gone into, or become aware of. This is why people continuously attract the same person just with a different body and look, because energy can only attract like energy.

This is why I say, the Universe is literally "you inverse." You are creating it all, the positive and the negative. Every person, circumstance, or event—past, present, and future—it's all coming from within you.

All of life lies inside.

Really pause and sit with this for a moment. I know this may hit hard, because we've all had people, circumstances, and events that we would never consciously call in, like a bad relationship. Think back to your worst relationship. What if that person was only "bad" because you labeled them that way? Instead of seeing them as "bad" or "wrong," what if you saw them and your relationship as *perfect*?

I'm not saying that you should have stayed with them or that there was no pain caused from it. No, I mean, what if your soul called in that partner to show you the ways you were unloving to yourself?

What if that person was there to show you how you weren't honoring yourself, that you weren't listening or trusting yourself, or respecting or standing up for yourself?

What if this person was actually one of your life's greatest teachers, and yet, because you've been resisting this potential reality, you have never allowed yourself to learn the lesson that they were called in to help you master?

When we think back on our most challenging relationships, most of us can point to a red flag or some sign we blew through and never listened to or did anything about. Sometimes it's that we never spoke our truth, set healthy boundaries, or even walked away when we knew we should have, and as a result, pain happened.

And yet when we start to see this, how the energy within creates our lives without, then that is when our transformation begins, when we allow ourselves to see that we are either a victim or a creator. We can't be both. It's one or the other, and the way to awaken our highest self is to realize and become aware that we've mostly lived in victim consciousness, blaming everything and everyone outside of us, and yet that gets us nowhere.

When we can go back and realize that we were a co-creator in even the worst relationships, that's when our lives can change forever, because we go from victim consciousness, which blames, to creator consciousness, which accepts responsibility.

LIFE IN LOW VIBRATION

To alter our destinies forever, the first step is to discover what are the energies within that are creating our lives on the outside. To change our lives on the outside, we have to change the energy on the inside first.

After I found out about my assistant, I became very focused on learning more about how the energy within calls in the people and experiences outside of us. It was only a few months after the incident with my assistant when I did a mushroom journey. Every year, around my birthday, I will sit in ceremony with plant medicine, and that year I wanted to go deep, *real* deep. The facilitator started by giving me a standard dose for a spiritual journey, which is about 3.5 grams. For context, a microdose, which is becoming more popular, especially for treating mental health conditions, is much less, approximately 0.3 to 0.5 grams.

Around this time, I was also beginning the process of peeling away my identities. I was seeing more clearly all of the tricks of separation, and how I had wrapped my identity in things like my career, my belongings, and even my marriage. So I was seeing all of this during my journey, and I was being shown how preoccupied I still was with how others saw and felt about me. So much so that after my wife and I got divorced, I was determined for everyone to see us as the "healthy and evolved" couple. As a result, I would invite her to events.

During my journey, I was confronted with questions that penetrated my heart.

Did you invite your ex-wife because you have had the time to heal and go through the process of energetically detaching from one another, or is she here because there is still something inside of you that feels guilt and shame over the divorce, and you need to please her? Is she here because you need to feel special, like you have access to all the answers, and you want everyone here to look up to you?

These questions were deep, yet I felt wonderful. It was like I was being shown parts of myself that I had wanted to see but had felt too afraid to face. I was about halfway through the journey when I asked one of the facilitators for more. I needed to go further within. He looked at me, looked at the mushrooms, then back at me.

"It's okay," I told him. "I'm ready."

So he gave me more. I knew what I was about to undergo with this higher dose—a massive ego death. And that's exactly what happened. I went deeper into my unconscious. Suddenly, my body started vigorously shaking, and I saw a specific word—*shame*—then my body shook as I felt something release or break off me, and my body went into a calm state.

What the hell was that?

Then it happened again, and another word—*guilt*—appeared, and my body started shaking uncontrollably until something released or broke off again and I grew calm. This process kept happening until it got to the point where I knew what word it was before it appeared, and so I started shouting them out.

"This is fear! This is apathy! This is grief!"

I cycled through every negative emotion—or energy—that a human being can carry. Apathy, shame, guilt, grief, anger, fear, comparison, judgment, victimhood, control, hopelessness . . . it was all there, and as I went through each of them one by one, I began to see each emotion or energy as a puzzle piece. As one piece fell off, it revealed the next.

As I was nearing the end of my journey, I saw a white circle of light waiting for me, and it was calling me to it. With each puzzle piece that broke off, I moved closer to this white light, and I realized that once I let go of all the pieces—all of that negative energy—I would die.

This is when I came to understand the term *ego death*.

It wasn't going to be a physical death, but a death of the self and returning back to oneness. The self is the ego, it's the part of our mind that keeps us in a state of resistance, fear, and separation. That part can only exist when negative energy is alive inside of us because its frequencies, like apathy and anger, guilt and grief, control and comparison, fit together like puzzle pieces to create our ego. When those energies fall away, then there is nothing for our ego to hold on to, nothing for it to identify with, nothing for it to feed off, and so it has to die.

Realizing this, I felt afraid, because a part of me—my ego—didn't want to go. And then I understood, I saw it so clearly that when my ego died, it didn't mean that I would die. No, I could still choose to be here on Earth as a new version of myself. So the "old Danny" would die, and the new me would be reborn.

So I chose to stay.

At that moment, I knew that I—or my soul—had chosen to be here on Earth at this time, in this body, and I was here for a reason. I'm telling you from my heart to yours, that whether it feels like it or not, you're here for a reason too, and like me, you chose to be here at this precise moment in time, in your body.

I began walking around the room, and I saw two girls who had also journeyed with me, and I told them, "I'm going to go, but I'll be back."

What I was experiencing was so intense, and then another word came up—*barriers*. As with every energy before, my body shook as I released the energy of the word, and I started thinking about how many self-imposed barriers we live with. Barriers around what we think is possible for our lives, around who we let in, around what we allow ourselves to experience, around how we see ourselves, and even barriers between each other.

And then it hit me: *We have no barriers*. All of the barriers that we have are man-made, and essentially illusions we buy into.

I looked down at my T-shirt, and I thought about how even our clothes act as barriers. Once, long ago, humans didn't need clothes, but today we hide behind them. They are what keep us from fully seeing each other in our naked selves. As I connected these dots, suddenly I was overwhelmed with the intense energy of shame about my body, and I saw how I had carried it with me for most of my life. As men, we're taught to compare ourselves to other men, judging our bodies based on the size of our muscles, our height, and even how big our penis is. In that moment, I felt all of the shame that I had been carrying around my beautiful body—the thing that keeps me here on Earth and that houses my soul.

Realizing there really are no barriers except what humans have created, I walked into the middle of the living room, flung off my shirt, and dropped my pants. I stood there naked as the day I was born with my hands high in the air.

"We have no barriers," I yelled. Instantly, two friends rushed over, asking me if I was okay.

"I'm the freest I have ever felt in my entire life," I admitted.

That's when the final word appeared: *Danilo*, my father. I felt all of the separation and the barriers that I had energetically with him. I was shown how all of these negative mental and emotional barriers came from my wounded masculine energy—the part of me that was never shown love, leadership, or guidance by my father.

For more than 20 years, I had barely had a relationship with him. My parents divorced when I was 13 years old, and my mom moved me and my two brothers from our home in New York City to California, while our father stayed on the East Coast. Out west, my mom struggled to support us. We lived on welfare in a tiny, two-bedroom apartment in the ghetto—in a crime- and drug-fueled neighborhood. I rarely spoke to my father, never saw him, and as far as I was concerned, he had abandoned me.

There I was in this profoundly deep spiritual journey, feeling all of the anger and rage, resentment and sadness, which I had carried toward him for years. Everything that had separated me from him, I realized, separated me from my highest self.

I felt it all in my stomach. Unconsciously, I kept reaching down toward my stomach and making a motion like I was pulling stuff out and throwing it into the air. This was all energetic, meaning that when my body shook uncontrollably and I was making the pulling motion, I was literally shaking off and pulling out the energy from within. All of this was happening without my control. Think of it like when someone says something to you and it makes you cry. It's an involuntary release of trapped energy. The deeper you go into this energetic work, the more you'll come closer to experiences like this as well. Thousands of people have had life-changing experiences like this at AWAKEN events without any plant medicine at all using breathwork to help dislodge this stuck negative energy.

As this was all happening, I thought, *If I'm going to drop dead, I want to be outside with Mother Nature.*

So I ran out of the house, and there I stood barefoot on the grass, my arms thrown wide open, my back arched, and my head tipped up toward the sky, and I shouted as loud as I could, "Danilo!"

And as my father's name left my lips, I felt all the energies associated with him—the anger, resentment, abandonment, sadness—leave my body too.

* * *

About three months after my journey, I was lying on a beach in Colombia when I thought back on my journey and everything that had happened. I started to realize that all the energies that had come up, broken away, and been released vibrated at low frequencies. And all of them vibrated at a level that matched the life that I was living before my mother died and I had gotten divorced.

It was the energies of apathy, shame, guilt, grief, desire, anger, fear, comparison, judgment, victimhood, control, and hopelessness that had caused me to be in the relationship that I was in. It's what caused me to be in the business that didn't fulfill me. It's what caused me to be overweight.

All of these energies were living inside of me and were keeping me from my highest self.

When we're in low-frequency energy, it stops us from moving forward. These energies feel heavy, like we're weighted down, confused, or indecisive, and when we do take a step forward, they pull us back.

I couldn't help but notice how much my life was changing just in the three months since my experience releasing all of that negative, low-frequency energy. It even led me to take a backpacking trip to Colombia by myself—something I had never done before. I had no plan, I was simply there being free, and that alone was a symbol of my newly found freedom and all of these barriers being gone. I was simply in flow, living life to the fullest.

When I first start working with people, I like to begin by focusing on three low-frequency energies that almost everyone has activated within them. When we get to Part II, we'll look at how you can begin to heal and clear any low-frequency energy from your body. For now, I just want to help you become aware of what's within that has likely created your life.

The Energy of Shame

I know the energy of shame well. When the housing market crashed in 2008, I went so broke that I couldn't afford groceries. When my son's birthday came, I couldn't even afford a cake, that's how broke I was. I value my role as a provider for the people in my life. I provide not only for my family—my wife, children, and even ex-wife—but my employees and friends as well. If you're around me, you're covered.

So for me to not be able to even buy my son a cake sent me deep into shame. Yes, I did wonder, *Why has God punished me? Why is "He" angry at me? What did I do to deserve this?*

Best-selling author and research professor Brené Brown has spent decades studying shame. She defines it as "the intensely painful feeling or experience of believing that we are flawed and therefore unworthy of love and belonging—something we've experienced, done, or failed to do makes us unworthy of connection."[1]

I love her definition, and I'd add, based on my work coaching thousands of sexual trauma survivors, that the energy of shame often comes from something that has been done to us that makes us feel ashamed of ourselves.

When we're in this frequency, we are often withdrawn. We feel unworthy at the deepest level, unworthy to even be alive. We often avoid eye contact. For some of us, when we have sex with our partners, we can't look them in their eyes, because we're afraid of the intimacy and connection. We're afraid because, at one time in our lives, we were shown that intimacy and connection leads to pain.

Shame can cause us to feel inherently flawed, thinking something is wrong with us, and that we have to be perfect to be loved or accepted. This can show up in relationships, in friendships, even at work. During a monthly support call in one of our programs, Monica talked about how she would completely shut down when her boss gave her feedback on her work, because she felt ashamed. She only felt ashamed because that energy hadn't moved out of her body yet.

When it remains activated, shame often causes us to become immobile. We literally cannot move forward in our lives. That's because we feel so unworthy of even taking action. At the core, we're afraid of what could happen, of making a mistake, or of the consequences if we move.

When shame is present on the inside, then we become limited—our potential becomes limited. We won't go out and date because we feel unworthy of being loved. We won't travel on our own because we feel unsafe. We won't tell our partners what we need or how we feel, because we feel insecure expressing our truth and being seen. We won't earn as much money as we could, because we never take the actions needed to put in for a promotion, start a business, or say no to the low-paying or disrespectful clients.

None of this is you.

Before we go any further, I want you to realize something. I want you to have the courage to accept into your heart that anything you hear in your mind other than "you are beautiful, abundant, prosperous, lovable, and worthy," or anything positive like that, is *not* you. If you hear anything negative like "I'm unlovable, unworthy, undeserving, or bad," that is coming from the energy trapped inside of your body.

As soon as you clear that energy from your vessel, which is your body, then it begins to open wider for you to receive more of God's light, more of life's experiences, and more of everything you want in life.

At your core, you are worthy. You are beautiful. You *are* love. And the reason you don't know this or can't feel this truth is because the energy of shame is activated.

Low-Frequency Energies

When we live in separation, we may activate numerous low-frequency energies, including:

- Anger
- Anxiety
- Attachment
- Blame
- Desire
- Disrespect
- Doubt
- Frustration
- Grief
- Guilt
- Impatience
- Perfectionism
- Poverty
- Pressure
- Pride
- Regret
- Resentfulness
- Sadness
- Self-loathing
- Shyness
- Worry

The Energy of Guilt

This energy typically causes immense feelings of self-punishment that we can't stop. Jasper, an entrepreneur, told me that he'll ruminate on mistakes he's made at work for days. It will even keep him up at night. "My co-founder and I met with potential investors, and I screwed up the presentation," he said. "They turned us down, and it was all my fault. I couldn't sleep for weeks. I'm such an idiot and a loser, and I feel like I've let our entire team down. It was as if my greatest fear had come to life."

What if the screwing-up of the presentation happened solely to prove to Jasper that the story, and in this case, the energy of guilt that lived inside of him, was true? What if screwing up the presentation was simply the energy that manifested in Jasper's real life? And what if that situation was exactly what Jasper needed in order to see what was activated inside so he could then go in and begin the journey of releasing it?

Are you starting to see how powerful energy actually is?

In my own life, I experienced guilt and self-punishment in many ways—with drinking, with porn, with food. I'd vow to eat a healthier diet filled with real, whole foods only to have that collapse a few weeks later, leaving me riddled with shame.

Maybe it's not food or porn for you; maybe you see the energy of guilt alive with your children, in your relationships with your parents, friends, or at work. What happens on the outside will look a little different for each of us, but the energy within us is the same. To see if it's activated within you, look for all the people and circumstances in your life that constantly make you feel guilty, even the people you blame for "making" you feel that way.

What if they were simply a scapegoat and a deflection, a way of avoiding the ownership for your energy? Behind this is the answer to everything you've ever wanted in life.

I say this lovingly, for anyone who feels the energy of guilt, which is truly most of us. As you heal the wound that created that energy in the first place, whatever habits or self-sabotaging patterns you have will naturally start falling away. Yes, even the way you interact with the people in your life, and even the people in your life—all of it will change when the energy within gets released.

The Energy of Desire

If you find yourself always chasing the next thing, then the energy of desire is alive. It's the idea that if we can only attain something, become "successful," get rich, get married, have children, buy a beautiful home, or have the perfect body, then we'll have it all. No more stress, fear, worry, and even better, we will *finally* be happy.

This is the energy that many, if not most, "successful" people have used to create their lives, including entrepreneurs, business leaders, celebrities, and influencers. Society has bamboozled us to look up to all of these people who seem to "have it all" on the outside, yet could the outward success actually be pointing to inward dissatisfaction?

When we create our lives from the energy of desire, nothing will ever satiate us. Life will always feel disappointing, like something is still missing, and that God continues denying us.

Not only did I live this energy, but so many people who I've guided through the years have too. Their businesses might thrive, money might flow in, they might have millions of followers on social media, or be plastered on the big or small screen, but the deeper within I take them, the more they realize not only are they not happy, but they don't really know who they are or what they actually want.

CREATING LIFE FROM VICTIM CONSCIOUSNESS

When we live in lower frequencies, we live in what I call *victim consciousness*, a disempowered state where we believe life happens to us. It's when we live in resistance—fighting against people, life, ourselves, and the Universe. When we make everything that has happened in our lives either right or wrong, good or bad. In this state, we judge ourselves, and we compare ourselves to others and what they have that we don't.

In victim consciousness, we give away our power to everything and everyone outside us, blaming situations, circumstances, and individuals for why our lives aren't how we want them. We'll use words and phrases including:

- "I can't help it."
- "This always happens to me."
- "It's not fair they did this to me."
- "If only they [partner, child, parent, boss, co-worker, friend] would change. They're the reason this is happening to me."

Take our partners, for example. We'll constantly blame them for the state of our relationship. We'll call them names and put labels on them like narcissist, manipulator, or gaslighter. Victim consciousness makes us believe we're unhappy in the relationship only because of what our partners have done to us. Yet the deeper we go, the more we realize that absolutely nothing in the relationship can exist without us having co-created it.

It's the same idea when it comes to our health, body, relationships with our children, parents, or friends, career, even our finances. Victim consciousness points the finger outside. If we don't have the money we want, it's the economy, the president, what's happening in our industry, or the stock market, our bosses, business partners, employees, customers, and clients to blame.

There's an unconscious payoff for staying in this state—we get to avoid all responsibility, because this energy tells us it doesn't matter what we do, the world is against us. We'll think, *Why even attempt to change our lives if nothing will work out, or when it's just going to lead to disappointment and more pain?*

So we don't even try, and as a result, we stay in the frequencies that feel comfortable and familiar. We perceive this as "safer." Yet this traps us in a loop of inactivity that comes at a terrible cost—more pain. Something inside is calling to us to awaken and release the energy of separation and low frequencies, but we keep resisting, which creates its own pain. Then the double-whammy of low frequency and victim consciousness that keeps calling in the same cycles and patterns, which also cause immense suffering. So we make money and lose it. We attract the same partners who make us feel unlovable or taken for granted. We stay in jobs where our bosses and co-workers disrespect us, and we allow our kids to take us for granted.

Deep down, we don't want any of this. It's just that we're stuck, and we will stay exactly where we are until we start releasing the lower-frequency energies and victim consciousness within.

THE ONLY PLACE TO LOOK LIES WITHIN

Are you beginning to see it now? That it's not the world outside of you that's causing your experiences—it's the energies within you. Can you feel how the thoughts you think, the choices you make, the actions you take, and even the people and patterns you attract are all shaped by the frequencies you're living from?

The great news is that when you heal and release the lower frequencies and victim consciousness within, you heal your life on the outside.

When you shift the energy, you shift the life.

When you shift the energy, you shift the life.

And the very fact that you're beginning to see how all of this works, to feel this truth in your body, marks a sacred shift out of victim consciousness into something more.

Welcome to your awakening!

To awaken is to become aware of a deeper truth—that maybe life hasn't been happening to you. That maybe, just maybe, you've been creating it all along. And not through willpower or vision boards or affirmations, but through the energy underneath every thought, every emotion, and every action you've ever taken.

You want to change your life? It's not about doing more. It's not even really about what you do, it's about the energy you do it from. Because the truth is, you can build a business, find a partner, and lose weight, and still carry the same low-frequency energy. When you create life from these energies, then whatever you attain won't last or fulfill you. Until you change the energy within, you'll keep re-creating the same patterns with different faces and different outcomes.

Most of us have spent our lives creating from low-frequency energies. Shame, guilt, grief, fear, insecurity, scarcity—these are the default settings of a world rooted in separation. But this isn't about blame. There's no guilt here, no judgment. You were born into a system designed to operate this way. The world teaches you to look outside of yourself for validation, for self-worth, for power. So of course you learned to live and create from that place.

But now, you're remembering, and once you see how it works—once you understand that your outer life has always been a reflection of your inner energy—you unlock something extraordinary: *the power to change it all.*

Because it's never been about how to make things happen. It's never been about the "how to" of business, love, or health. It's always been about *the energy* behind your actions, about the energy underneath all of your thoughts and emotions.

Change the energy and you change the actions.

Change the actions and you change the outcome.

AWAKEN YOU
Awareness Prayer

Right now, you're probably becoming aware of energy and experiences, and starting to see how the two connect. For many of us, it can be scary and overwhelming, so I invite you to enter these moments of awareness by placing both hands on your heart. In the silence within, say the following:

"I am aware of [insert person/circumstance/event/energy] now. Please show me how to heal this energy and release it from within me. Please bring me the guidance, help, and circumstances to heal this [insert person/circumstance/event/energy] and change my life."

You can also say:

"God, I am scared, because I know what this means. I know a part of me will have to die. A part of me that I have lived with will have to die, and I am afraid to let go. Please be gentle with me. Please help me to release and let go of that part of me that no longer serves me into the love and light of all that is and oneness. Thank you."

The journey back to your heart, back to your highest self, and back to oneness starts with *deciding* that you are ready to release everything that's been holding you back or blocking you from your highest self.

CHAPTER 3

LIFE IN COHERENCE

My spiritual journey led me to believe that money, wealth, and possessions were "bad" or "wrong." I had been so wrapped up in materialism and needing things outside of myself to validate me and make me feel good that when I realized this, I swung hard in the opposite direction. I gave away all my designer suits. I sold my flashy house and got rid of my fancy cars.

Because I had made them all from the "wrong" energy, I wanted nothing to do with material possessions except for the most basic.

Flash forward six years, and it was time to get a new car. My business was thriving. I was remarried, and my wife, Jen, and I had an almost two-year-old beautiful little girl. I was thriving. I felt joy, love, and inner peace the likes of which I had never experienced.

In that space, I found myself suddenly pulled to driving a luxury car again. But right away, my mind jumped in: *What are people going to think? I'm a spiritual teacher. Shouldn't I deny all material possessions? Isn't materialism "bad"?*

I decided to play small, so I went to the dealership and test-drove an older, safer model. But the minute I climbed behind the wheel, everything inside of me said no. So I went in to hand back the keys, and I saw the most glorious, new Bentley Continental I had ever seen.

At that moment, I thought back to the very first expensive car I ever bought. I was 27 years old, and I was trying to prove to the world that I mattered. Back then I believed a car would make that happen, that it would show people I was worthy of respect.

When I stood in the dealership gazing at that new Bentley, all of those memories flooded back.

This car is too much. You're not that guy anymore, I told myself. I wasn't the person who needed a nice car to win other people's approval, to feel worthy and deserving, and to prove myself.

So I walked out of the showroom and climbed into my old car. That's when it hit me: I really wasn't that person anymore, because *the energy* of who I was being had shifted. I didn't need the car. I wanted the car. I wasn't in fear, operating from lack. I was in love and tapped into true abundance. I was an abundant *being*. The car? It was just an outward reflection of the inner abundance I now was. And so I walked back into the dealership and said yes to the car my heart actually wanted.

CREATOR CONSCIOUSNESS

At first, I was saying no to the car because I was afraid to allow myself to love something nice. I was afraid of what everybody would think of me as a spiritual teacher if I drove something expensive. I realized that was just fear talking.

There is a whole other world that exists, a world where we finally live in and honor our authentic self. And when we do, we're finally free to create and receive from our heart's purest expression. We can have the car. We can live in the dream house. We can wear what we love and eat what we desire, not because we need any of it to feel worthy.

Because we already are worthy.

What I'm describing is the journey that awakening your highest self will move you toward when you leave separation, victim consciousness, and lower frequencies, and step into oneness, creator consciousness, and higher-vibration living. If victim consciousness is about disempowerment, then creator consciousness is its opposite twin—an empowered state where you blame nothing and no one outside of yourself for what has happened in life. Instead, you *know* and embody the fact that you are the creator of your life's experience—all of it.

Rather than seeing life as happening to you, you see life through the lens of "it's happening *for* me." You understand everything in life is here to teach you. It's for your benefit and for your life's journey toward oneness.

This state grants you vision for your life, which you can align with action, so you move forward with clear intentions and clarity. That's self-leadership. You are the leader of your life, not someone or some system outside of you. You trust in yourself to lead you. And you know that even when you're not headed straight, you'll find a way back on the path, trusting that everything is here for your divine purpose (even that detour and stumble).

Ultimately, you trust in life.

In victim consciousness, you fight against everything—yourself, your partner, life, the Universe—as if you were in a boxing ring, trading jabs and trying to beat it into submission. In creator consciousness, life is your partner, one you can work with instead of fight against.

No matter what happens, you know you'll be okay. This perspective changes everything, because when you're in victim consciousness, you often don't act for fear of the consequences, outcomes, and the perceived pain that accompany them.

In creator consciousness, there's nothing to fear, not even pain, because *everything serves a purpose.*

Take that toxic relationship or person in your life. What if their "soul" purpose was to come into your life to cause you the exact pain you needed to feel, so you would learn to stop bypassing red flags and your intuition? What if they were here to show you parts of you that were ready to be released? Maybe it's the part of you that puts others first? Maybe it's time you put yourself first. Time to speak up for your needs or to put healthy boundaries down that say, "No, I love and respect myself too much to allow you to talk to me or treat me that way, so we're done."

Victim consciousness never allows you to even think these thoughts. Creator consciousness does.

When you're in this energy, you also have emotional mastery. You feel everything and honor your emotions, yet they do not rule your life, they're its compass. When something uncomfortable or difficult arises, emotions give you the access point to get curious and explore versus running from it. As a result, you'll ask questions like

"What is this emotion here to teach me?" and "What is coming up to be healed?"

You also know that everything you want in life—*you are*—and so you can attract it all. And yet you're not attached to when or how it shows up. People in victim consciousness are so attached to how things "have to be," they'll try something, and if it doesn't work, even in the slightest, they'll race back into the box and say, "See, I knew it wouldn't work. I knew it couldn't be this easy."

In creator consciousness, you'll try something, and if it doesn't work, you'll say, "That's okay. I'm one step closer to . . ." or "Every no gets me closer to a yes," or "There's something here for me to learn."

This shows up in relationships too. You no longer cling to others or try to control them. You're unattached. You don't need the relationship; you *want* the relationship, because you see the value in being in it. And when it's time to release a relationship, you will. Trusting fully that it has served its purpose.

This is the energy which you embody. As a result it's your attitude and approach with *every* experience in your life.

See, in creator consciousness, you stop outsourcing your power to anyone or anything. You no longer blame your past, wait for permission, or try controlling reality—you collaborate with it.

You understand you are the author of your experience, and whatever that experience is, you created it. This is when you begin leading your reality from within, understanding that your frequency shapes your world and as such you protect it. You no longer allow negative energy from people regardless of title or position. You no longer allow unhealthy or toxic food to enter your body. You live from a place of understanding that thoughts, emotions, and beliefs—conscious or unconscious—are creative instructions to the Universe.

The beautiful thing about creator consciousness is that it takes what has happened in life and says:

> *I will no longer be imprisoned.*
>
> *I will no longer be a victim.*
>
> *I will transmute the pain, I will transmute the energies, and I will create life.*

I will create life where there once was pain, and I thank the pain.

I will create life where there once was death, and I am grateful for the death.

I will create life where there once was fear, and I thank the fear.

I will create life where there once was separation, and I bless the separation.

When you have activated this energy, you no longer see yourself as separate from God or life; you see yourself as one with it all. When you're one with all that is, you are one with all you want, and you realize there is nothing stopping you from experiencing and creating the life you've always wanted.

A HIGH-FREQUENCY LIFE

Regardless of what you've experienced in life up until now, here's the great news about it all: Just as you can create life from lower frequencies, you can also create it from higher frequencies! As we begin our awakening journey, I like to focus on three high-frequency energies that we can activate, or begin moving toward.

HIGH-FREQUENCY ENERGIES

When you step into creator consciousness, you also activate high-frequency energies, including:

- Abundance
- Acceptance
- Altruism
- Compassion
- Courage
- Forgiveness
- Gratitude
- Joy
- Love
- Letting go
- Peace
- Presence
- Resourcefulness
- Surrender
- Willingness

The Energy of Courage

Courage is the energetic bridge between all of the low- and high-frequency energies. It's what helps move us from fear and victim consciousness into love and creator consciousness. It's what *allows* us to open our hearts when they were once closed, to face what we once feared facing, to let go of the pain that we've held on to our entire lives, and to try what we've always feared trying.

Courage is not the absence of fear; it is the presence of Self—the real Self. It's the moment when we decide "I will no longer avoid," and we start facing everything we've buried deep inside keeping us blocked and in fear.

It's leaving the relationship our soul knows has come to an end yet fear has been keeping us in. It's starting the business we've always wanted to start, setting the boundary, speaking our truth, listening to ourselves over others, asking for guidance, and looking within for the answer.

This frequency has a voice, and it's different from any of the lower ones. When fear says, "What if I fail?" courage asks, "What if I succeed?" When fear questions before we act, "How will this work out?" courage says, "I'll take aligned action first, knowing that the how will appear eventually."

Tap into the energy of courage, and everything in your life starts changing—not instantly, but it's a start. Where fear never allows your transformation to begin, courage accepts that life is a journey and allows the process to unfold. With every step you take, you begin realizing that everything you've ever wanted in life has always been in the place where you've been terrified to look: on the other side of fear. And the only way you can see through it is by tapping into the courage to face what you fear the most. When you do, you realize, that thing you've been afraid of? It's actually been the portal to your life's greatest transformation all along.

The Energy of Acceptance

After courage comes a deeper, quieter shift, one that doesn't look too dramatic on the surface yet causes profound internal changes. This is the energy of acceptance. It comes after, because it requires courage to fully embody it.

In this frequency, we stop fighting with what *is* and waiting for what isn't. It's the energy that moves us from seeing everything as either right or wrong, or good or bad, to simply seeing everything as is—without judgment.

This isn't about giving up or saying that everything is fine when it clearly isn't. It's about letting go of the need to force change in life and in others in order for us to find peace, realizing that the only place to find it is within us.

Most people spend life resisting reality and fighting with life, wishing something in their past or present was different, or that something never happened. Yet the energy of acceptance teaches us to stop wishing for a different past or present. This is a critical step in awakening our highest self. We cannot heal what we still reject or fight against, and we can't move forward if we're still trying to undo what has already happened or wishing that it never did.

On an energetic level, something magical begins to happen when the energy of acceptance gets activated: Resistance to life as it is, to what has happened in our past, and what is happening in our present, ends, and with it all struggle.

We cannot heal what we still reject or fight against, and we can't move forward if we're still trying to undo what has already happened or wishing that it never did.

Acceptance is the energy that allows us to finally end the war with life and everything that has ever happened in ours. It leads us to begin to see and experience the beauty in life as we leave the protectiveness of our mind and ego, and our heart begins to reopen. And as this happens, our body softens, and the mind starts to finally quiet.

As such, acceptance is the doorway to returning to our feminine and the ability to receive all that life has to offer us.

This energy sounds like:

- "It happened and I survived."
- "They hurt me, yet I learned a lesson from the pain."
- "I thought my life would look different by now, yet here I am, and I'm grateful to be here."

When we have activated acceptance, then we no longer need the past to change in order for us to heal. We no longer need other people to be different in order for us to feel peace. And we no longer need to fight against the present reality in order for us to feel happy.

Instead, we meet life, the past and present, where it is, allowing everything to be what it is.

When you meet your life, at this exact moment even, with presence, you will discover something sacred: You were never broken by something that happened to you in the past. Nothing you went through, no decision you made (or didn't), no experience you encountered was ever wasted or even wrong. Even your darkest chapters were simply a necessary part of your becoming.

And so acceptance is not the end of transformation—it's the beginning of deep, inner peace.

The Energy of Peace

Peace is the silence within us that is untouched by people, circumstances, and events. *Nothing* bothers, triggers, or moves us in this energy. The common preoccupations of society, the pull to pay attention to what's happening in the world, or the ever-so-present back-and-forth on social media over someone we don't agree with simply cease to exist. Peace isn't something we go get, it's something we uncover, because it's always been there beneath the chaos, the trauma, the anger, and all of the stories that we've held on to for as long as we can remember.

Peace is *surrender,* not the kind that comes with giving up. The kind that comes from giving in to life, to love, to now. As such, right and wrong, past and future, even life and death, disappear.

In the energy of peace, everything simply is and it's perfect.

We stop needing to understand everything, needing to fix everyone, needing to become someone different than who we are, because we realize: "I already am perfect, exactly as I am, and I always have been," and "They are already perfect, exactly as they are, and they always have been."

When we're in this energy, we'll say things such as:

- "I don't need to prove anything anymore."
- "I trust life, even when I don't understand it."
- "I am exactly where I need to be."
- "I forgive the past, release the future, and meet this moment fully."

When we embody peace, our energy becomes medicine for everyone around us. We enter a room, and others begin to breathe deeper. They feel safe with us. Not because we're trying to do anything, because we simply are, and in this state, we soothe, calm, and help others activate peace within themselves.

We are no longer at war with ourselves or life, so there's nothing to defend or protect against, not even our beliefs. We have ours and others have theirs, so there's no reason to convince anyone else to think differently or be different than who they are. There is also nothing for us to hide, so not only are we fully transparent, but we allow ourselves to *be* our authentic *self.*

If this energy sounds passive, I assure you, it's not. It's one of the strongest on earth, because it can't be moved by anything outside of it. In peace we do less and create more. We speak less and say more. We want less and receive more.

Peace is the reward for those who have had the courage to walk through the fire and *laid it all down*—their fears, separation, and victim consciousness. It comes to those of us who've cried the tears, faced the fear, loved through the pain, and finally said: "Enough is enough. I choose to let go, I see myself for who I am, and from this day forward I choose stillness and peace in my authentic self, in my highest self, in my connection to oneness."

When we're in peace, we're basically *unf*ckable-with.* No thing, no person, no experience disturbs our inner peace. In fact, we don't even notice all the "strife" in the world. That wild remark the U.S. president made? *What remark? What president?* The stock market plunges or soars. *What stock market?* Politics, the economy, racism . . . *what are you even talking about?*

There is no "God forbid, I'm mugged," or "God forbid, my spouse gets cancer." And if something does happen, we know in our heart and soul that life is perfect, that everything is perfect. In peace, we understand that everything has to play out as it does in order for us to become who we are meant to become.

This is something Carolina was learning. She had an ex-boyfriend who kept showing up in her life, asking for favors, and pleading with her for help.

"Do you smoke crack?" I asked her.

She laughed. "No, of course not."

"Why don't you? I bet it's because you know it's not good for you. Maybe the pipe looks pretty, but you always pass, because you know the damage it will do to you internally, right?"

She nodded, smiling.

"So in this way, you consciously avoid the pain the crack is meant to cause. You probably don't even find yourself in situations where people are smoking it, do you?"

"No, I don't even think about it," she said.

"Of course not. Well, isn't your ex like crack?"

Silence. I could see her searching for what to say, before responding, "Yes, but when he calls me, I really do want to see him."

"No, you actually don't," I challenged. "That's the energy inside of you talking. It's the energy of worry, insecurity, and fear you'll be alone for the rest of your life that's been activated. And the ex is being brought to you so you can finally see that part of you and go on a journey to release and heal it. So you can learn to stand up and honor yourself. So you can start the process of reactivating the energies of peace and acceptance within.

"Until you do this, something will always happen. Every reason in the world will show up, trying to entice you to take a hit from the pipe. So your ex will wind up in the hospital, texting you, 'Please, help me.'

"When you're in the energy of peace, if you even see this text, your immediate response will be 'No, it's crack!' And the same way you stay away from crack is the same way you will stay away from your ex."

Nothing can faze us. The toxic ex has no power over us. The assistant who steals causes us no harm. The big work contract or job that disappears leaves us shrugging our shoulders, smiling, and thinking, *Thank you. Next, please.*

The energy of peace means we know—and feel—how beautiful and perfect life truly is.

IN THE LIGHT OF LOVE

High-frequency living is very simply the energy of *love*.

It's not a thing you focus on doing. It's more what you become, the natural outcome of the work—or the healing—you do.

But this can be a bumpy journey.

When you're in lower frequencies, who you have become is the manifestation of fear, since that's the dominant energy within. And it's that state that keeps you in a constant state of resistance with life. If it's true that energy attracts energy, then what do you attract more of? The same things in life that match the frequency of that fear.

What starts happening, as you go on this journey is that you begin leaving the fear of the mind, and you begin entering the love of the heart. But you're not used to living with an open heart, and at first that scares you. It's the unknown and the uncomfortable, and so, very naturally, your heart will close, and you will rush back to your mind, the place that feels safest, but only because it's what you're used to.

You'll go back and forth between fear and love. Back and forth. Back and forth until one day, you realize:

The secret to living in the safest way possible is actually the opposite of being in fear. It's keeping your heart open, no matter what.

The more you keep your heart open, the more you're in love. And the more you're in love, the more you will call in what vibrates at that level. Eventually, you'll ask yourself, *How was I ever afraid of love? How was I ever afraid of what I truly am?*

This is when the real lesson starts. That's where you get the opportunity to face everyone in your life you hold judgment, anger, or resistance toward, and you get to say, "What is this energy doing for me? What's the impact this has on my life? And is it allowing me to keep my heart open?"

Because if it's not, and you now know that "like calls in like," then what is the anger, frustration, hurt, pain toward this person, situation, circumstance actually doing to you? It's keeping you in a state of fear, which only attracts more fear.

So what is the only option you have? Well, if a life of true abundance is what you want, then all that's left is to send love out into the world—specifically, to whoever or whatever has caused you the most pain.

It's to open your heart to that person, event, or situation. It's to forgive. It's to understand no one person or situation actually did anything to you. It's to understand that everything and everyone was actually a perfect embodiment, a necessary reflection, of the energy within you.

That person, event, or situation came into your life and played the perfect role, which caused you to feel and experience everything you needed to feel and experience, so you could reach this point, right here, where you get to choose the beauty of loving it all in spite of it all.

This is the pathway to becoming one with the creator itself. Because after all, isn't the creator love? It's the moment when you realize everything and everyone who ever caused you to feel pain were actually your greatest teachers. Because with the pain comes the opportunity to accept, forgive, and return to love.

And if fear and low-frequency energy is here simply to teach you—to hold up a mirror for you—then what is there to fear?

Nothing, because it's all happening for you. Whenever you feel fear, here are five things to remember to bring you back to presence and peace:

1. It's not going to happen (98 percent of our fears never actually come true)
2. If it does happen, it's because my soul called it in
3. If my soul called it in, that means there's a lesson in it for me
4. If there's a lesson in it for me, that means my soul is trying to advance
5. If my soul is trying to advance, well then, the highest point of advancement is a life of peace, love, and abundance

So as a result, there is nothing to be afraid of.

Always remember: The more you open your heart, the more in love frequency you are, so the more love you will attract. The more you attract love, the safer you actually are.

When you reach this place, you're free. Free to create and live the life you truly want.

PAIN	GIFT

AWAKEN YOU
The Gifts in Life

Now it's time to begin the journey of surrendering, and you're going to tap into the energy of courage to begin the process of letting go and releasing the low-frequency energies. Use the two columns on page 60 or draw them in a notebook. Under "pain," write everything you've been judging in your life as bad, wrong, or painful, then on the right-hand side under "gift," jot down the gift it's given you or the lesson it's taught you.

For example, I had parents who didn't know how to show me love. It actually taught me how to tap into the energy of resilience. Maybe like me, you've gone through a tough relationship, and the gift was that it showed you what you actually want in life. There are no right or wrong answers here, nor any good or bad ones. Simply listen within to what's coming up for you and write it down. This act alone begins the process of beginning to *trust* in yourself and life.

PART II

HEAL

CHAPTER 4

THE JOURNEY OF LIFE

I've always been a dreamer.

My very first dream was to find "the one." Since I was 12 years old, it was all I thought about. Every girl I would meet, I'd wonder, *Is she the one? What about her? Is this it?* I wanted it so badly that I first got engaged in my early 20s. We were wrong for each other in *every* way, and fortunately, we called off the engagement. I knew it was the right thing, yet I felt terrified. *What if I never find the one? What if I'm alone the rest of my life?*

Around the time I turned 27, I really wanted to settle down, get married, and start a family. All I could remember was how much pain I had felt in my last relationship, and I just wanted to meet someone who was the exact opposite of my ex-fiancée. And so when I did meet that woman, I was like, "That's it! She's the one!"

There were times when it felt like something was off, but I ignored it. In fact, I didn't know those were my feelings and intuition trying to communicate with me. I was so disconnected from myself that I didn't know how to listen to my feelings, so I bypassed them. I felt this deep need to get married, not to mention, I felt the pressure of society. *This is what everyone is supposed to do,* I thought, so I got married and finally achieved my first dream.

My second dream was to buy my mom a house. When my parents divorced, and my mom moved my brothers and me from New York City to California, I instantly stopped being a child. My dad wasn't around. He stayed in New York, so I became "the man of the house."

For example, I was the one who did all the driving in my family. In the City, you don't need to drive, you can take public transportation everywhere. In California, it was different, so I convinced my mom to buy a car.

Except I forgot a minor detail . . . she didn't know how to drive.

She bought a stick shift, which made it even worse. Every time we got to a stop sign, or the street was slightly elevated, the car would start rolling backward. My mom was such a nervous woman too, and popping the clutch scared her. She looked terrified behind the wheel, and I hated seeing her like this, so I decided I would do the driving.

I convinced a neighbor to teach me how, so at 13, I was the one carting my family around town. What can I say? It was the 1980s, I thought I could get away with it, and I did. I also acted like a father to my younger brothers, taking them to their sports practices and going to their games. In a weird way, my mom stopped being my mom around this time, and I became like a partner to her, because all of this responsibility for our family was thrust onto me.

So with all of that came this belief that it was up to me to change our lives.

When I graduated high school, I realized no one was coming to save us. My dad certainly wasn't, and the government assistance we were living on at the time meant we were dead-ass broke. All real change in life starts with a decision and a crystal-clear vision, and mine was simple: I decided I was going to buy my mom a house.

The vision? I had the audacity to believe I would move us from the worst part of the city to the best by the time I was 21. Guess what? By 21, I had done it. I bought my mom a house, and as a result I stumbled across an industry that would change my destiny forever: real estate.

This led to my third dream: starting my own business and becoming a real estate millionaire. I started as a real estate agent, and I made great money until the housing market crashed in 2008 and I lost *everything.* From that experience, I vowed to make a comeback, but this time, I would open my own real estate company, become a broker, and one day reach $1 billion in annual sales.

You see, the thing about making a decision and giving it your all is you learn something priceless: You can do it.

That sends a message to your subconscious mind. It creates a new story within yourself that says, I do what I say I'm going to do, and I can achieve what I set my mind out to achieve. So 10 years after the opening of my brokerage, I realized all of those dreams too, and we reached $1 billion in annual sales.

From there, I kept racking up all the "wins." The car, home, career, business, money, family—I had it all. Yet something was always missing.

I'd go to these motivational events every year and sit in the first or second row. I'd fill out whatever worksheet the presenter gave to help us balance our money, family, and health.

I thought I had done *everything* right. I had achieved everything—the ultimate purpose—that society had told me I needed to have a good life: a beautiful wife, wonderful kids, a giant home, a massive business, lots of money, influence, everything. So why didn't it feel good? Why did it still feel like I was out of balance? And why did I still feel empty inside?

WHAT WE *THINK* PURPOSE MEANS

Like me, you have been bamboozled to believe that your purpose in life comes from doing and achieving. You were taught by society to create goals such as finding a partner, getting married, starting a family, building a successful career or business, buying a beautiful home, driving a nice car, and making sure your body looks a certain way.

This is all very masculine in energy, all about doing and going. When the masculine is wounded, there's always somewhere else you have to be, something else you have to strive for and achieve, and always some destination outside of yourself that you have to get to. Now, there's nothing wrong with this, until you start asking yourself deeper questions like: *What am I giving up? What am I sacrificing? How do I actually feel within?*

The problem is that if you're only in your masculine energy, you're only in your mind. If you're always on the go, when will you ever be still?

If you always have to be *there*, then how can you ever really be *here?*

If you always have to be there, *then how can you ever really be* here?

If you're constantly in a state of determination and seeking, then how can you ever be in your heart, intuition, feelings, and your feminine?

This is what leads to feeling lost in life. You keep endlessly searching outside of yourself, believing that your purpose in life is to check off boxes and attain achievements, possessions, and accolades. It's not.

Your real purpose in life is to heal your soul and return to your authentic self. The part of you that needs nothing, that is at peace with what is, has nowhere to go and no one to become, because you are here now, being you, and that's all there is to *be*. There. That's it. That's your purpose.

I can hear you thinking, "Okay, Danny, that sounds good, and what do I *do*?" I get it. That was me too. I wanted to know *every* step and every action I had to take. At first, learning that our soul's purpose is to evolve into a state of enlightenment is not going to be enough. That's because most of us live in our minds, and our minds need a game plan, a destination, and a specific outcome.

Except returning to your authentic self and "arriving" at enlightenment is quite the opposite. There is no doing. It's just remembering who you were before the pain, before the letdown and hurt, before the guardedness, and before you felt like you had be someone different to receive love.

See, when we're in our hearts—in our feminine energy—then we understand that purpose can't be about doing, because if it is, then when will we ever rest? When will it all ever stop? When will the number in the bank account be big enough, the house be fancy enough, or the body be beautiful enough? When will we ever experience inner peace? When will we ever share love, opening ourselves to receiving and giving it?

When we look closely, we see that real love can only be given by also receiving. Receiving comes when we allow, and allowance comes when we stop and allow ourselves to rest, trust life, and be still. So purpose can't be about what we're here to do and attain.

It's about who we're here to be and become.

LIFE AS AN INTUITIVE, ENERGETIC BEING

So who are we here to be and become? Our highest selves. To "do" that, we must return to our hearts. But what drove us from them in the first place? Yes, it was separation as we talked about in Chapter 1, and there's a deeper truth it's time for us to explore. In this chapter, we're retracing your energetic steps that led you out of your heart and feminine energy and into your wounded, unconscious mind and masculine energy.

For many people, the topics we're about to go into bring up some intense feelings. So take your time, pause whenever you need to, and remember to breathe slowly. Know, too, that you can always take a break by putting down the book and returning to it later.

Now, let's dig in.

Underneath every drive, goal, or need all of us have to achieve something in our lives—be it finding love, career success, or owning nice things—is the same truth.

All any of us are looking for is love.

We are desperately, and unconsciously, seeking that sense or feeling of being in stillness, peace, connection, and oneness. And where was the one place, the one time, when we actually felt this in our lives?

It was when we were in our mother's womb.

Imagine for a moment what it must have felt like being in darkness, connected to your mother, where you had everything you needed: nourishment from the umbilical cord, protection from the outside world, and total safety to grow and develop. Did you have anything to do, or could you simply *be*?

Then you were born, and you left the dark, which is feminine, and entered the light of this world, which is masculine, and for the first time, you knew fear and separation because you were no longer connected. Where you once felt safe and secure, you became utterly helpless and defenseless. You needed your mother, and your father if he was around, for *everything*. Your very survival depended on them. You needed to be fed, protected, and cared for. This is where you first learned that life equals "outside-in," in other words, it's where you learned on an energetic level that what you needed to be whole and complete was *outside* of you.

Now, pause.

You came into this world as a powerful, intuitive, and energetic being, meaning that you could sense or feel the truth of something beyond the logical, rational, and without proof or evidence. We all come into this world like this.

You arrived here as a clean slate, and immediately you started intuitively picking up on the energy around you, especially what was coming from your parents or whoever cared for you.

Your intuitive, energetic powers don't come online when you can legally drive or when you turn 18. These are gifts you, and everyone in this world, are born with. Society, religion, and darkness don't encourage us to develop these gifts. In fact, they'll probably tell you that being an intuitive, energetic being is evil, New Age, demonic, or crazy. All part of the plan to keep you in your mind. I believed that for many years, because that's what I was told. Yet what I discovered was, when I went into everything I was told to avoid, I found myself.

Embracing your abilities can become a pathway to returning to your authentic self and allowing guidance, messages, and inspiration from God, the angels, your spirit guides, and the Divine to come through. Every human being has the ability to tap into and receive healing and guidance from above, we've simply forgotten.

Now, what do you think you wanted to do when you saw your parents or caretakers in pain?

You had just come from love, and so you did what anyone who loves someone wants to do: take away their pain and stop their suffering. It's what any parent prays for when our children are hurt. We would gladly take away all their pain and suffering and make it our own, if we could, because we love them so much.

That is exactly what happens when you're born as the intuitive, loving baby that you were. You wanted to take away the pain and suffering of your parents, so you absorbed whatever wounds were activated within them.

Most of the low frequencies and victim consciousness running your life—from doubt to worry, blame, shame, and desire—aren't even yours to begin with. That energy originally came from your parents, their experiences in the world, and the energies inside them. They unknowingly passed those on to you, the same way their parents passed it on to them. This happened when you were in your mother's womb too. You were downloading generational feelings, emotions, and energies from the beginning.

THE BIRTH OF THE UNCONSCIOUS, WOUNDED MIND

I know my mom loved me; she loved me so much. As a single mother, she worked hard to take care of us, always putting mine and my brothers' needs before hers, yet she didn't know how to express that love to me. How could she? Her mom wasn't around to give her the blueprint of maternal love.

For the first two weeks of my life, my mom was also not physically present with me. After delivering me by C-section, she had to stay in the hospital, because she was at high risk for serious complications—this was in the '70s. So I didn't have my mom caring for me at first, just my aunts and my dad.

The truth was my dad didn't know how to be a dad either. He didn't know how to be in his masculine energy, because he had never had a father who demonstrated that for him either.

Right away, I was energetically picking up that something wasn't right, because the fullness of love wasn't really available to me. I didn't receive what my heart yearned for, and I have a hunch that in some way, you're a lot like me.

For a moment, imagine yourself as a baby, lying on your back, completely defenseless and dependent on your parents or caretakers. Now picture yourself lying there, looking up to see your parents or caretakers. In those early years, all you're looking for is love, safety, nourishment, and protection. So what do you think happened if, instead of feeling the energy of love, you felt the energy of anger, disconnection, stress, or anxiety? Or maybe you felt the energy of favoritism, that a parent, or parents, seemed to love your brother or sister more?

Now take a deep breath, because the following sentences could bring up some memories or emotions you weren't prepared to deal with. Just hold your hands over your heart and say to yourself, "I am a safe place," and know that you are not alone in this moment.

What do you think happened if, instead of receiving love, you received abuse—emotional, mental, physical, even sexual—from your parents?

What if your mother prioritized your father, a boyfriend, or another man over you? What if she wasn't there for you? What if she was an alcoholic or an addict, or she struggled with mental health issues? What if she bypassed your emotional needs or constantly spoke negatively to you, dismissing your goals or desires as a child because deep within she didn't believe—not in you—but in herself? What if your mom didn't know how to show you love the way you needed it?

And what if what I just described all came from your dad? What if instead of having both parents, you only had one or none?

When you don't get your needs met in the way you need them, if you don't feel love, and instead you're manipulated, abused, or abandoned, then your mind immediately steps in to protect you, as *you* are the priority. Since this is happening to you as a child, then the mind is stepping in from a wounded place, because you aren't prepared to deal with or understand why these things happen, especially not from the two people who were supposed to love you.

So what does the mind do?

It creates a story.

It creates meaning out of the pain—because as children, we can't just feel pain and let it pass through us. We don't yet have the emotional tools or the spiritual maturity to say, "That wasn't about me. That was their wound." Instead, we internalize it. We turn the pain inward. We begin to shape our identity around what happened—not because it's true, but because it feels safer than the raw truth that our needs weren't met by the people we loved most.

And so, the child begins to build a world that makes sense to them—a world that helps them cope, survive, and feel some sense of control. And this is where so many of our unconscious patterns are born. These early defense mechanisms—these invisible survival strategies—end up shaping who we become as adults, until we bring them into the light.

Let me show you what I mean.

If a child senses that love must be earned, they might become the achiever—the straight-A student, people-pleaser, or over-performer. They learn that their worth is tied to performance, so they work tirelessly to be perfect, successful, or "good" believing that if they just do enough, they'll finally feel loved. If this sounds familiar, you got it, this was me.

If a child feels unsafe or emotionally overwhelmed, they might become the caretaker. They focus all their energy on keeping others happy, managing emotions, smoothing over tension because on some level, they believe their safety depends on other people's moods. They might grow up believing it's their job to fix, please, and save. Take a wild guess the kind of partners these people attract as adults in relationships?

If a child is constantly criticized, ignored, or made to feel "not enough," they might become the invisible one. They learn to shrink, disappear, and to keep their true thoughts and feelings hidden—believing that being seen is dangerous. These children often become adults who apologize for existing, who fear rejection, and who struggle to take up space.

If a child is violated, betrayed, or abused, they may become the controller, someone who tries to manage every detail of life, because they've learned that letting go leads to pain. Underneath their desire for control is a deep fear of being powerless again.

Some children become the rebel—acting out, breaking rules, defying authority. Not because they're "bad," but because they're angry. Deep down, they're screaming, "Do you see me now?"

Others become the chameleon. They read every room, shapeshift to fit in, adjust themselves to avoid rejection. They've learned that who they really are isn't enough or that it's too much.

And some children simply become the helper. Always available, always putting others first. Because they've been taught—directly or indirectly—that love must be given, not received.

Undoubtedly, one or several of these examples might connect with you. If they do, it's important to understand that these identities aren't who you are; they're who you became to survive. They were brilliant strategies, crafted by a wise little soul doing their best in an environment that didn't feel emotionally safe. But here's the truth:

What helped you survive then is often what blocks you from thriving now.

What helped you survive then is often what blocks you from thriving now.

Because as long as those unhealed energies remain within, you will keep creating the same patterns in your adult life. You'll keep attracting people who reinforce the original wound. You'll keep re-creating situations that echo the original pain. Not because you're broken—but because your body, mind, and soul are still trying to resolve what never got healed.

Yet this is the beginning of true healing. Not trying to fix yourself, but beginning to understand *why* you became who you became. Deep, transformational healing happens when you start to become aware and look back on yourself and your past with compassion, not blame. It happens when you begin seeing your story clearly, without judgment, and when you give yourself the space to feel the pain that was never safe to feel, allowing it to move through you now, with love.

Once you see the story, you can heal it and begin to write a new one.

The Original Story

Are you beginning to see how in those first few days, weeks, months, and years a program was being written? A script was being downloaded into your subconscious, crafted by your wounded little mind and designed to help you survive and to keep you safe in a world it believed was dangerous.

In the process, your mind created stories about yourself, about love, about life, about what is possible and impossible for you, and even about God.

What are these stories? They go something like this. The more love you received as a little boy or girl, the more you were allowed to fully be you. The more you were shown exploring and discovering life on your terms was not only safe but rewarded, the more unstoppable you feel in life, because love fills you, anchors you, and it programs you with a deep sense of worth, confidence, and safety.

The opposite is true too. The less love you received, the less safety, warmth, or emotional presence you were given during those formative years, then the more you will move through life searching for it, looking for it outside of you in validation, success, attention, relationships, and things. The less love you received, then the more limited you will be in what you believe is possible in life, not because it is—but because your energy still carries the story that "love is unavailable to you."

If you felt the energy of fear, stress, or anxiety from your parents, then your subconscious mind registered a very simple message: "Life is not safe. Life is stressful. Life is uncertain. Life is a struggle."

And when I say "life," I mean all of it—relationships, love, money, health, career. *Everything.*

As a little boy or girl, religion hasn't gotten a hold of you yet, either. It hasn't programmed you with any stories, so you don't have a perception of God. In your mind, who do you think you saw as God?

It was your mother and father.

Your father is literally the masculine representation of God, and your mother, the feminine representation. Energetically, they're the first experience you have of God—or love—in human form. So if your mind felt abandoned, rejected, or unloved by either parent, the unconscious story it created was that God (love) is not safe.

God (love) can't be trusted.

God (love) abandons us.

God (love) is angry.

God (love) doesn't love me.

Can you see how deep this is? If your mother, in her wounded energy, was anxious or fearful, your mind may have created the story that the feminine—your heart, your intuition, your inner knowing—is also unsafe. That the feminine cannot be trusted. That being soft, being still, being vulnerable will get you hurt. So you disconnect from that part of yourself. You push down your feelings. You stop listening to your intuition, you override your body's wisdom, and you harden.

The same idea is true with your father and your masculine. If your father wasn't present, if he abandoned the family emotionally or physically, or if he was unpredictable, angry, or abusive, your subconscious may have created the story that the masculine is unsafe. That leadership, action, structure, and confidence are dangerous. So you may struggle to lead, to plan, and to trust yourself. You might hesitate to take action or to stand in your power, because deep down, your mind believes that masculine energy hurts people or can't be trusted.

And so these wounded energies begin to live within you, quietly, invisibly, yet powerfully. They become the background frequency of your life, shaping how you love, how you create, and how you see yourself and the world around you. Without realizing it, starting in childhood and continuing into your adult years, you will attract people and experiences to match those early frequencies. You'll keep repeating the same patterns over and over—different names, different faces, yet it's the same energetic story. You'll find yourself feeling confused, frustrated, and heartbroken, wondering why, no matter how hard you try, things feel heavy and your life unfulfilled.

You might chase the things the world told you would make you feel worthy—money, status, relationships, beauty, success. Or maybe you won't chase anything at all, because somewhere deep inside, you've accepted the story that you don't deserve it. That you're unworthy, and that love, abundance, joy, and peace just aren't for you.

For example, if your mom or dad were constantly stressed, your mind may have crafted a story that stress is normal—so you create a life filled with it. You find yourself overwhelmed in your relationships, in your job, in your finances, in your health. Not because you want stress, but because it feels familiar and safe.

If you learned that love was unavailable from your parents, you'll spend your life searching for it outside of yourself—just like I did. You'll chase love through marriage, possessions, money, validation. You'll try to prove that you're finally "good enough," hoping it will fill the void left behind.

If your parents struggled financially, and the energy of lack filled your home, your mind may have created a story that says, "Life is struggle." And so no matter how much money you make, you'll always find a way to struggle. You'll sabotage it, feel guilty for having it, you'll lose it, or fear losing it constantly—because abundance doesn't feel safe.

If there was fighting or abuse in your home, your mind may have crafted a narrative that says "love means pain" or "closeness means chaos." So you'll attract relationships that mimic that dynamic, or you'll push away love altogether because deep down, your mind believes love will hurt you.

In my case, my mind created a story that love was unavailable to me and that it had to be earned. If I just made enough money, had enough success, looked a certain way, or got married, then I'd be worthy of love. So I went out and tried to prove I was worthy of love, trying to earn it through achievement. I looked for it everywhere—except where it actually lives: inside of me.

My friend, this is why I do this work. This is why I'm writing this book, because I spent 44 years of my life this way, and no one ever told me it was all because of the energy within. No one ever told me the connection between my energy, my parents, and the life I was living. I'm pretty sure no one ever helped you connect the dots either, because no one teaches us how this world really works.

I'll never forget a conversation I had with a Hollywood actress over lunch one afternoon. She told me she was tired of getting passed over—tired of always coming in second and never getting the A-list, starring roles. I gently asked her about her relationships, and she leaned in and lowered her voice and said, "For the last ten years, I've been the mistress to one of the biggest actors in Hollywood."

So I asked her, gently but directly, "As a little girl, where did you learn that when it comes to love, you will always be in second place?"

She froze. Her eyes opened wide as if a code had just been cracked. Tears welled up.

She told me about her childhood, about growing up with her younger brother who had been very sick. Her parents had poured most of their time, energy, and attention into caring for him. She loved her parents deeply, and she knew they loved her too. Yet energetically, she still carried the wound of being passed over, of being unseen, and of not being chosen. So her unconscious mind had turned that wound into a story that said: "Love means second place."

Without even realizing it, she had built a life where the energy within her kept her living out that story.

Still second in relationships.

Still second in her career.

Still second in her own heart.

Like me, like the Hollywood actress, you too are living out a story that your wounded mind created in childhood to try and keep you safe. The specific circumstances may change, but the pattern remains the same, and you will keep living out the same stories, attracting the same patterns and people, until you go within and heal the energy that created it.

The Story of "Never Again"

Sometimes, the frequencies we absorb as children don't just create pain, they create a vow. A silent promise that says, "Never again. I'll never feel that pain. I'll never be that powerless. I'll never feel that small or unseen or not enough."

This was me. I didn't build a massive business and make more money than anyone in my family because I absorbed the energies of inspiration or desire from my parents. It was the opposite. I grew up in a society that told me, based on how I looked, that I was "less than" others. And my parents—God bless them—carried the heavy energies of shame and unworthiness, passed down from their ancestors, from their culture, from where they came from, from being told in silent and loud ways that they didn't belong.

I picked up that energy and absorbed it, and my wounded mind created a simple yet powerful, unconscious story:

"Life is a fight."

We don't chase goals—we chase the energy we were missing.

We don't chase success—we run from the wound we never healed.

So I fought to win. I believed that if I wanted anything in life, I'd have to go to war for it—because the world, my parents, even God wasn't going to hand it to me. I became obsessed with the idea of proving myself. I hustled, pushed, and performed. I was going to be successful, make tons of money, and be seen, respected, and admired by everyone. I was going to own the car, the house, the watch, the brand, the image, not because I was shallow, but because deep down, I never wanted to feel shame, disrespect, or rejection ever again. I never wanted to feel less than anyone else.

And that's what we all do, in our own ways.

We don't chase goals—we chase the *energy* we were missing.

We don't chase success—we run from the *wound* we never healed.

Now, let me be very clear: building a business, making money, creating success, none of it is wrong, evil, or bad. Yet when we create from our *wounded minds*, there will always be something missing. No matter how much we achieve, we will often feel or sense a quiet ache in the background, following us through our days. A whisper in our soul that says, *"This isn't it. Something's missing. There's something deeper I'm meant to feel."*

And that "more" isn't out there.

It's within.

OUR CHOICE. OUR WOUNDS.

One of the most sacred steps we can take on this path back to our highest self is to begin healing our *mother and father wounds.* This starts when we awaken to a deeper truth—one that the mind might resist, yet the soul remembers. This is another "take a deep breath" moment, as this one is probably going to cause some pain, anger, and resistance:

Your soul chose your parents.

Take another deep breath, especially if you feel something stirring deep within. That feeling, whatever it is, is the very energy we're here to look at, release, and free ourselves from.

And, yes, this part of the journey can be difficult. As I mentioned before, for many of us, the pain we carry runs deep. Some of us have been hurt, abused, neglected, abandoned, and violated—physically, mentally, emotionally, and sexually—by the very people who were supposed to love, protect, and nurture us unconditionally.

We're conditioned to not talk about this, but here's the thing dark energy doesn't want you to know: Speaking the truth sets you free. Naming the pain removes the energy of secrecy, and it dissolves shame, guilt, and fear. When you bring what was hidden into the light, the healing begins.

So what if your soul chose your exact path? That just like I did, your soul selected its parents, its lessons, and even its wounds? Is it possible that maybe—just maybe—everything that happened to you in childhood and until this exact moment has been happening *for* your evolution, not your punishment? And maybe the only thing that's been keeping you from seeing the gift in the pain is the story your mind created to protect you from it?

Your parents were not a mistake. They only appear that way when you're trapped in victim consciousness, where everything in life happens to you instead of for you. When you stay in that state, believing your parents were a mistake and resisting, fighting, or struggling against your past, it keeps you from the path your soul is here for.

When you are in creator consciousness, your parents were the perfect messengers, carrying the exact codes and lessons your soul needed to grow, awaken, and return to wholeness. In creator consciousness, the pain trapped within them and transmuted into you becomes your greatest teacher and the pathway to freedom in life. You needed the pain to discover peace. Without the wound, there is no healing. Without the absence of love, you don't remember the truth of love.

I've come to see that every wound my parents carried was a gift to me. My grandfather wasn't a father to my father the way he needed him to be, and so my dad developed a stutter that made it hard for him to speak his truth. That pain pushed me to perfect my voice, which gave me my career and eventually led me to my life's calling. Because of my father's masculine wounds, it put me on the path to healing my masculine wounds, and it was the very thing that taught me forgiveness.

My mom lost her mother when she was just 13 days old. That absence of the feminine, of nurture, of emotional presence, lived within her, and she couldn't show me love the way I needed, because she had never been shown it herself. That disconnection to the feminine led me to search for love my entire life, and ultimately, to surrender when I couldn't find it outside of me. That surrender became the start of my healing. When my mom passed away from lung cancer, a disease deeply connected to unprocessed grief, it forced me to go deeper than I had ever gone before. Her death cracked me open, dismantling everything I thought I believed about God, religion, and life. And it gave birth to the journey that brought me here. That brought you here, and that created this moment.

If my mom hadn't died, then you wouldn't be reading these words.

And what if—stay with me now—before we came into this life, my mother and I made an agreement?

What if she said to me, as we were still in spirit, "I'm going to go down first, and I'm going to lose my mom, so I disconnect from love and the feminine. This will cause me to carry grief within me that I will never resolve, and I will eventually die from lung cancer at an early age. Do not worry or fear, because my death will awaken something in you. It'll set you on a journey to discover who you really are. And when you've healed, when you've returned to your heart, and you've remembered the truth about yourself, life, and God, then you'll find real love, and I'll return."

I know this is going to sound really woo-woo, but in several journeys, both Jen (my wife) and I have been shown that my mother has returned—as our daughter. So the love my mother and I never knew how to give each other then, we'll give to each other now.

Can you feel how beautiful that is?

Can you feel how something like that might be happening in your life? Don't think with your mind, feel with your heart and soul. Move past all the stories and limiting beliefs society and religion have programmed into you and feel how maybe, just maybe, all along everything in your life has been . . . perfect.

Society doesn't want you to remember this. It wants you disconnected. Because if the connection between you and your mother is broken, so is your connection to the feminine, to love, and to God. And if that connection is broken, the child (you) retreats into the mind. And a child stuck in the mind is easy to program, easy to manipulate, easy to control. Society doesn't want you to ever understand this because it wants you to hold on to the grudge and the anger and the resentment that you have toward your mother and your father.

Because the anger and resentment you have toward your mother is the anger and resentment you have toward your feminine, toward yourself. It blocks your capacity to receive, soften, love, and trust your intuition. So it keeps you in your mind constantly thinking and never connecting within, thus never receiving from above.

And the anger and resentment you have toward your father is the anger and resentment you have toward your masculine, toward yourself. It disrupts your ability to lead, take action, and feel confident and safe in your authentic self and power.

Finally, the anger and resentment you have toward both your parents is the unconscious anger and resentment you have toward God and life itself. How can you create all that you want from life when you unknowingly resent and resist the actual creator of life?

Pause here. Close your eyes. Feel what's coming up. This is not small work. This is the sacred work of a lifetime.

If you're searching for your purpose, this is it. It isn't what you do—it's what you *heal*.

It's your mother wound. Your father wound. Your feminine wound. Your masculine wound.

When we let go of the energies we've absorbed, when we surrender the stories our wounded mind created, we awaken our soul, free ourselves, and, finally, come home.

And from that place, we can create anything and everything our heart and soul desires. It's not coming from fear, survival, from lack, or from doing. We're creating life from truth, love, alignment, and from *being*.

When we can say with our whole heart, "I chose this. I chose my parents. I chose my wounds, so I could transmute them and return to love," something shifts. A door opens, as the past no longer owns you. The pain no longer defines you. And life becomes yours to create.

So close your eyes. Place your hand over your heart, and ask yourself:

Which version of the story feels truer?

That life is random and your suffering was meaningless?

Or that everything—every tear, every wound, every loss—was part of your soul's awakening?

I'm not here to tell you what to believe. I'm here to help you remember what your soul already knows, if you choose to allow it.

As you read these words, it's possible you feel some resistance rear up, maybe in a big way. That's the tricks of the mind working to hold on. Remember when I told you about my moment with the pastor, when I had to decide if I was going to live in fear or love? Well, this is another moment like that, when you're being asked to tap into courage so you can surrender the stories, the limiting beliefs, the energy, and let go.

Because this isn't just about your past. It's about your power.

And that power, my friend, has always lived inside of you.

AWAKEN YOU

Remember, Release, Return

You've come a long way in this chapter. You've remembered and faced things you may not have thought about in years. You've felt what was buried deep within, and you've allowed yourself to start the process of seeing where it all began

Now it's time to bring it home. To begin the healing—not in your mind, but in your body, in your breath, and in your energy. This is where your transformation begins.

So take a moment to find a quiet space, and place one hand on your heart and one on your belly. Close your eyes, and begin to breathe slowly, deeply, fully, in through your nose for four seconds, then hold for four, and then release your breath through your mouth for four seconds. Then hold for four more seconds.

Now, repeat three more rounds like this, allowing your nervous system to begin settling, and your body to soften.

Gently bring into your awareness the image of your mother. Don't force anything. Just allow whatever version of her to arise, whether that's her face, energy, or presence. Without judgment, just feel what comes up.

Now, silently ask her from your heart: "What energy did I absorb from you that was not mine to carry?"

Wait. Listen. Feel.

Maybe it was fear. Maybe it was shame. Maybe it was grief, anxiety, or resentment. Whatever it is, just notice it—without needing to change or fix it.

Now, with a heart full of compassion, say the following—aloud if you can, or in your mind if you need to:

"Mom, I forgive you. I now release the energy I absorbed from you that was never mine to hold. I honor your pain. I honor your journey. I thank you for my life, yet I choose to release

this energy in love for its highest good and the highest good of all, and I now call all my energy back to me, every speck and every chunk, from wherever it is, I call it to me now."

Envision your energy coming back to you, and *feel* what shows up for you. Allow your body to do whatever it needs to—wiggle, cry, shake—and when you're ready, affirm the words:

"I choose freedom. I choose peace."

Breathe that in.

Now repeat this exercise with your father. Bring his energy to mind, and feel into the emotion, without judgment.

And ask:

"What energy did I absorb from you
that I no longer need to carry?"

Feel it, and allow the truth to rise, before saying:

"Dad, I forgive you. I release the energy I took on from you—consciously or unconsciously. I honor your wounds. I honor your humanity. And I no longer need to carry your pain. I choose to release this energy in love for its highest good and the highest good of all. And I call all my power home."

Now place both hands over your heart and repeat:

"I forgive. I release. I return to love."
"I forgive. I release. I return to love."
"I forgive. I release. I return to love."

Let the words sink into your body. You may feel emotion rising—allow it to move through you. You may feel nothing at all, and that's okay too because nothing is also something. Know that this is the beginning of a deeper integration.

Now take three more breaths. Long. Slow. Deep. And when you feel ready, open your eyes.

You've just taken the first step in healing your mother and father wounds. You've moved from unconscious memory into conscious release. You've begun the journey from victim to creator. This is the work that changes lives. This is the path that leads you home.

It would be my honor to personally guide you through a process of remembering, releasing and returning. To access this, go to **dannymorel.com/RRRmeditation**.

CHAPTER 5

HIDDEN WOUNDS

When I married my first wife, I knew deep down we weren't right for each other, yet I still went through with our wedding.

After my mother died, and I got honest with myself, I knew we needed to end our marriage for both our sakes. I felt like it was my shot. *If you're going to do something, do it now,* I thought.

But I was quite honestly a little bitch.

I couldn't say to my wife, "I want a divorce." I couldn't even talk to her about what I was feeling. I couldn't assert or honor my needs. And I couldn't give her the love she deserved, needed, and was worthy of. This wasn't new to me. I had spent my entire life bypassing my own heart and my authentic self. Not once had I stopped to really ask my heart, "What do you want? What are your dreams? What excites you? What makes you happy? What do you love? What is your truth?"

When it came to my career, I did the same thing. The only reason I got into real estate in the first place was because I heard I could make a lot of money. When I was 18 years old, I asked a real estate agent if I could work for him for free, just so I could learn the business and buy my mom a house. In my first year, I made $100,000. No one in my family had ever made that much money before. From there, I just kept doubling my earnings, selling more homes each year, and going all in on real estate.

But did I ever stop and ask in my heart, "Do I like this? Is this what I want to do?"

I did this with my marriage too. I hit the age of 27, my career was in full bloom, yet I wasn't married, and I wanted to be. I never paused to really ask in my heart, "Do I actually want to get married, or am I just in love with the idea of getting married?"

My situation wasn't unique. So many of us are bypassing our hearts, whether it shows up in our relationships with our partners, children, parents, and friends; in our careers and jobs; and in how we care for our bodies. Instead of listening and honoring our hearts and highest selves, we lean on religion, society, family, and everything external from us to tell us what we should do with our lives, the decisions we should make, and even what we should want in life.

So why do we do this? Why do we bypass our hearts?

A DANCE WITH ENERGY

To understand why we bypass our hearts, we must begin our story at the dance with energy happening within each of us. At the core of everyone is a back-and-forth movement between two powerful forces: *masculine and feminine energy.*

This isn't a new idea. We can trace the idea of two balancing energies to spiritual traditions including Hinduism, which has a positive and negative power and deals with duality, and Taoism, the ancient Chinese philosophy that gave birth to the yin-yang symbol. In Taoism, yin (right-brained, intuitive, creative, and fluid) represents feminine energy, while yang represents masculine—left-brained, structured, clear, and ready to move.

Traditional teachings often explain yin and yang as opposite and complementary forces. I prefer to see them as partners, as two sides of the same breath, two halves of the same whole.

Masculine energy is connected to our mind, thoughts, and logic. It allows us to envision the future and set goals, and then motivates us to take action to realize them. It's focused, determined, and moves with purpose. Not to dominate, but to build, to protect, and to pursue life with integrity. Masculine isn't afraid of emotion. It knows how to hold space for feelings—ours and others'—without needing to fix anything. It's the energy of quiet strength, never needing to prove itself, because it knows in the depth of its being that it's strong, powerful, immovable, unshakable, and steady.

Masculine Energy Traits

- Light
- Yang
- Expanding
- Hot
- Mental
- Mind
- Consciousness
- Moving Closer or Further Away
- Upward Motion
- Active
- Giving
- Single-Focused
- Outer World
- Hard
- Will
- Assertion
- Hustle
- Outcome
- Destination
- Thinking
- Reason and Logic
- Strength
- Positive Polarity
- White
- Sun
- Fire/Air
- Spring/Summer
- Movement (Directed)
- Doing
- Linear
- Differentiating

Feminine energy balances the masculine. It is associated with the heart, intuition, connection, and emotions. It calls us to be present in our bodies and in time, not to escape doing, but to feel what's driving it in the first place. It's the energy of nurturing and also of fierce truth telling, guiding us to listen to our bodies, to honor our emotions, and to follow our intuition—that voice within, our deep sense of knowing right from wrong, yes from no, that comes before our mind can explain or rationalize it. The feminine is about *being* rather than doing, receiving rather than taking, allowing life to unfold rather than forcing it to bend to our will. It's our connection to ourselves, to others, to the earth, and to spirit.

Feminine Energy Traits

- Dark
- Yin
- Inward
- Contracting
- Cold
- Emotional
- Passive
- Receptive
- Body
- Feeling
- Multi-Focused
- Inner World
- Soft
- Trust
- Attraction
- Flow
- Process
- Journey
- Imagination
- Flexibility
- Negative Polarity
- Moon
- Water/Earth
- Autumn/Winter
- Movement (State of Flow)
- Being
- Circular
- Integrating

For love to exist, life must exist. For life to exist, duality must exist. And so within everyone exists masculine *and* feminine energy. For life to be lived abundantly, we need both energies, working in harmony, dancing together as partners.

Now, when I talk about masculine and feminine, I'm not talking about gender, which is about the physical form, and the biological, or outward identity. This is about energy, something much deeper, something that we cannot see, feel, or even touch. Energy is in how we move through the world, how we lead, how we feel, and how we love. Think of it as the current flowing underneath the form we take and the actions we make.

The journey we're all on in this life is one of *balance*. It's learning how to allow both energies to breathe, move, flow, and exist together in harmony. It's knowing when to lean in with strength (masculine), and when to soften with trust (feminine). It's knowing when to slow down, to listen, to open our heart (feminine), and when to step forward, to lead, and to protect (masculine). The goal isn't to pick one energy. That's old-world thinking, splitting the two apart as if they're in conflict. Masculine and feminine are just two expressions of one life force.

Like the yin and yang symbol, each energy holds the other.

When we start living from this balance, we don't have to force anything. We don't have to think about "how to be." We just *are*, and in that moment, the separation between the two energies dissolves, and they become one.

And as a result, we become one within and one with everything there is.

THE ORIGINAL "SIN"

Most of us live with unbalanced masculine and feminine energy. That's not a judgment. It's simply the nature of the human journey. To truly heal the imbalance and restore harmony, we must understand the original split. For many of us, that story begins in a garden.

Yes, *that* garden.

The story of Adam and Eve isn't just a religious tale. It's an ancient symbolic narrative, representing the moment that humanity became disconnected from our true spiritual nature. It is the metaphorical point when the divine balance between our mind and heart, our masculine and feminine, was broken.

Let's start at the beginning with the serpent.

We've been told the serpent was the deceiver, the evil one, and the reason we "fell." But in ancient mystical traditions, including Hinduism, the serpent actually symbolizes something else entirely: kundalini energy. In these traditions, it's believed that kundalini energy, which is feminine, lies dormant at the base of the spine, coiled like a snake. When activated, this energy will rise through the seven chakras—or energy centers in the body—moving from the bottom of the spine to the crown of the head, resulting in a profound spiritual awakening to our highest self and divine truth. Kundalini energy thus is connected to our inner life force, sacred transformation, and awakening.

Now, think about what this means.

A snake sheds its skin, just like you and I must shed our old selves to become new. But this kundalini awakening requires something we've been taught to fear: a deeper connection to pleasure. That's sexual pleasure, something most religions teach us is wrong, but also the pleasure of being alive, joy, and connection to earth and intuition.

This is where Eve comes in. She represents our feminine energy, our heart, intuition, and inner knowing. In the story from the Bible, Eve is portrayed as the deceiver of man. She eats the apple—given to her by the serpent—and she is blamed for all of humanity's downfall.

Let's look closer, because Eve follows her intuition. She chooses to engage with the serpent—with transformation, awakening, and her life force. She reaches for the apple, which grew from the earth (feminine), and she trusts the pull of her body and the wisdom of her soul. And what is she told after? That she has sinned. That she's wrong. That she causes the pain of the world.

That's where the hidden messages begin, and the spiritual programming we're still untangling to this day, which is symbolically that the heart cannot be trusted, that the feminine is deceptive, intuition is dangerous, pleasure is a sin, and the body is shameful.

Separation from our hearts, on an energetic and spiritual level, originated as a collective wound, a collective split, where humans left their hearts and split the feminine energy from the masculine.

Because Adam, then, becomes the symbol of our masculine energy—the mind. And what does the story of Adam and Eve from the Bible tell us about him? That Adam's gravest mistake was listening to the feminine (as represented by Eve). And so, the "moral" of the story becomes that our mind should never trust the heart. That the masculine should never follow the intuitive, emotional, instinctual wisdom of the feminine. That the heart is "deceiving." (Writing this pisses me off. Western religion has been keeping us divided, not just from each other as we talked about earlier, but from ourselves.)

The story of Adam and Eve is actually a story of division, and keeping us out of our hearts, fearing the feminine energy within.

Disregarding it as a result. And if this is how we relate to our own feminine, how will we treat the feminine in the world: our women?

Symbolically, Adam and Eve leaving the Garden of Eden represents the spiritual moment when the division was born.

It is when the heart was cast out (of the garden), and the mind was placed on the throne. When we went from being one to being separate. If we're separate within ourselves—within our feminine and masculine energy—then how will we ever be one with life and Source? We can't.

Breathe in this understanding, and let the energy within the story of Adam and Eve move through you. This is how the two energies, meant to dance in harmony within us, became opposites, clashing and fighting each other, imbalanced, distrustful, dominating or submissive, controlled or controlling.

And from that original split, the split within ourselves began too, and with it our suffering. Why? Because it's the heart that is the doorway to God—not the mind. The feminine is the vessel of spiritual connection. It's the access point to the divine, not the enemy, not something meant to be suspicious of, avoid, ignore, or fear.

Your ability to feel, to receive, to flow, to intuit, to surrender—that is what makes you whole. That is where your power lives.

But when you're told that the feminine is wrong, then you begin closing your heart. By the way, this didn't happen consciously. You didn't decide one day to do this. It happened on the energetic plane, which is deeper than most humans can access.

As a result, most of us simply live life as half of who we are, without ever consciously knowing that a part of ourselves is missing. From the moment we're born, most of us are taught to believe that the mind is the master, and so we live from the neck up. Then, when we're told that God judged Eve (or the feminine) and proclaimed consequences for her actions and Adam's for following her, we're taught to fear both love and God. Many of us even identify and call ourselves "God-fearing" men or women, and we grow up thinking and believing God is a punishing God. Absolutely nothing could be further from the truth.

My friend, now you know where this seed was first planted, when that beautiful dance with energies was stopped, and when you were taught to fear the feminine, the heart, the intuition within you.

And not just in you, in the collective consciousness of humanity, because what happens to a society that fears the heart, disconnects from the Earth, and suppresses the feminine?

We get exactly what we see now: a world ruled by logic without love, power without presence, action without alignment, and success without soul.

So if you truly want to heal and feel whole again, if you want to reconnect with God, with your intuition, with love, and with your power, then you must begin to heal the original split within yourself. The split between your mind and your heart, between your masculine and your feminine energies, and between Adam and Eve—within you.

This is the sacred work of returning to balance, of bringing the masculine back into the right relationship with the feminine, and of allowing the mind to serve the heart, not the other way around. This is about releasing the shame placed on your body, on pleasure, on sensitivity, on sensuality, on softness, and on your life. It's the sacred work of reclaiming your right to feel, to rest, to lead, to act and to live, not from fear, but from union. Not from separation but from oneness.

The serpent was never the enemy. The apple was never a sin. The earth was never the punishment. And the feminine was never the problem. The problem was the story we were told about all of it and the split that came as a result.

THE THREE PHASES OF ENERGETIC EXPRESSION

Alongside our collective split, each of us carries inherited hidden wounds from our parents. These are the roots of every negative pattern, story, limitation, thought, and habit that you wish you could break.

Let that land for a moment.

I want to be really clear this isn't about blaming our parents. They never knew these energetic wounds lived inside of them, and they did the best they could with what they had. Even if you were raised by parents who you'd say were loving and supportive, you probably still carry wounds to your masculine and feminine energy.

It must be this way, so you can consciously choose healing and balance where there was once pain and imbalance. So you can consciously choose love where there was once fear, connection where there was once disconnection, and oneness where there was once separation.

In life, our feminine and masculine energies express themselves in three very distinct ways, two of which, when we are wounded, show up as imbalances. I call these the *Three Phases of Energetic Expression*:

1. **Suppressed**: When an energy shuts down, shrinks, and disappears.
2. **Overcompensating:** When an energy becomes dominating, controlling, and exaggerated.
3. **Balanced:** When we have healed and restored any imbalances, so the energy doesn't control us, it moves effortlessly and with ease through us, as the beautiful dance partners they were meant to be.

We're going to walk through how these energies may show up in life. I encourage you to read each slowly, pausing, breathing, and letting them move through you. When something hits, go ahead and circle, highlight, or underline it. This isn't about judging how your energy is showing up. It's not about labels like right or wrong, or good or bad. This is about helping you to begin seeing your own patterns with new clarity and naming them. Once you can name it, you can consciously choose to keep it or let go and heal it.

Suppressed Masculine Energy

- Aimless and Indecisive
- Financial Instability
- Not Present
- Unprepared and Procrastinates
- Lacks Boundaries

Suppressed Feminine Energy

- Always Waiting
- Constantly Nagging
- Takes Everything Personally
- Blind to Red Flags
- Uses Invisibility as Protection and Is Codependent
- Needs External Validation

Overcompensating Masculine Energy

- Overly Aggressive, Quick to Anger, Violent
- Punishing and Abusive
- Paranoid and Jealous

Overcompensating Feminine Energy

- Smothering, Flies off the Handle, and Is Manipulative
- Impenetrable
- Bulldozing Boundaries, Judgmental, Suspicious
- Uses Sex for Extremes

Balanced Masculine Energy

- Confident, Moves with Purpose and Clarity
- Presence Through Consciousness and Self-Awareness
- Truth Seeking
- Safety, Protection, and Leadership

Balanced Feminine Energy

- Trusting with the Ability to Receive
- Connected to Intuition
- Strong Connection to Their Inner World
- Creative and Playful

The Quest for Balance

What came up for you in that section? How much did you underline, circle, or highlight? Were there profound moments of awareness, maybe even tears? Whatever came up, remember, it's all perfect as it brought you here to this moment.

To get to the healing, we need to acknowledge a hard truth: Wherever we go, our masculine and feminine energy goes with us—along with the wounds and imbalances we carry within them. Until we go in and begin to heal these imprints, they will follow us into every corner of our lives, from our careers to our health, finances, and even our relationships. It doesn't matter how much we accomplish, how many goals we hit, or how spiritual our practices are.

If the energy is off and imbalanced, the foundation will always feel shaky.

One important distinction to understand is that these imbalances in our masculine and feminine energy look different for everyone. How they show up for you depends on your unique story, upbringing, and the energies you learned to either suppress or compensate for. Some people feel it in constant burnout, while others will see it in anxiety, avoidance, or control. Some people feel it in the ache of never quite being enough, no matter how much they do or give, while others experience it in struggling to allow themselves to be seen and accepted as they are, never quite allowing anyone close.

Yet I know how important it is to show real-life examples of how these energetic imbalances play out in our lives. That's why at our events, we always create space for participants to share their awakenings and life experiences. There's power in seeing ourselves, at least parts of ourselves, mirrored in other people's stories. In keeping with the spirit at AWAKEN, I'm sharing examples of how masculine and feminine energy may look when it's suppressed and compensating. As you move through the stories, don't get too caught up in the surface details, as they may not match your life exactly. Instead, do your best to look deeper.

Ask yourself, what's the energy underneath? How might suppressed masculine and feminine energy show up in your life? In what area or areas of your life does this most prominently play out? Finances? Relationships? Health?

How does masculine or feminine energy show up when it's compensating? And in what areas do you see it most?

Be raw, real, and vulnerable with yourself, and you will find a mirror, and when you do, your truth will meet you.

Always on the Go

You can never slow down. You say yes to everything. Resting and relaxing? That's for when you're dead. There's always a new goal to chase, something to prove, something to conquer.

Does any of this sound familiar?

If it does, then you're likely carrying a wound in your feminine energy, because the feminine is the opposite of go, do, and get. Feminine energy is rest, receive, and allow. When there's a block in the feminine, there's a block in the heart. We stop trusting that life will meet us. We stop receiving freely, and instead we grip tightly. We push and constantly hustle, unconsciously operating from the belief that we have to make everything happen on our own. That it's us against life and against the world. Even if we go to church or have some regular spiritual practice, we energetically act as if it's us against God or the Universe.

What's happened is that we're overcompensating, swinging hard into our masculine energy. This expression needs to prove itself, and so the internal story and belief becomes:

If I do enough, win enough, succeed enough—maybe then I'll be worthy. Maybe then I'll feel peace.

This shows up in the workaholic, the perfectionist, and the one who can't stop. Constantly doing, constantly giving, constantly on. And here's the twist—the world actually rewards this behavior. Especially in the West, we glorify the grind, idolizing hustle and measuring our worth in output.

But when masculine energy is left unchecked in this overcompensating expression, it can become destructive, leading to burnout, exhaustion, and apathy. We lead a life full of doing, but it's often void of deep connection and meaning, and fulfillment.

Even when we know we're imbalanced, letting go of lifestyle feels terrifying. Why? Because stopping means slowing down. And slowing down means feeling, it means facing what we've been avoiding: the feminine, the emotions, and the heart.

It's why we're on the go in the first place, we're avoiding the pain the heart has been carrying. We've become so used to living in our minds, where things feel controlled and safe, that dropping down into the heart feels like a threat. Because if we go there, we'll have to face what we've been running from: the original wounds in our masculine and feminine.

Instead, we keep moving. We build businesses that demand our time. We attract clients who drain us. We take on roles in our personal and professional lives that keep us constantly needed. And we call it success, when, in fact, it's just survival, dressed up in productivity. When we're exhausted, and can finally admit to ourselves we are, then we often blame everything outside of us—our boss, our clients, our spouse, our kids, our parents, our friends, our co-workers, our neighbors, even the person in the grocery aisle with us for all the stress and strain in our lives.

But who's creating it all? We are.

And we will keep re-creating this energetic pattern until we finally stop and say, "Time out. I'm done running and avoiding, and I'm willing to sit still and go within to face whatever it is that I've been running from in the first place." Society may have told you this pausing is a weakness. But that stillness? It's the most powerful thing you can do, because that's where your real healing begins. When you stop and return to your heart, you meet the parts of you that have been trying to protect you all along, and the wounds that caused the rupture in your energy in the first place.

This was Alison's story.

For as long as she could remember, she had always been an overachiever, always hustling, and setting and crushing her goals, and doing everything "right." But in her early 40s, her body buckled, and extreme fatigue and burnout took over. It was so bad that she took a leave of absence from her job as a nurse—something that had defined her identity for years.

When I asked her what she learned about life as a little girl, she told me that her mom was also a nurse, whom she remembered as either always working or sleeping. And when her mother was awake, she often seemed overwhelmed or angry. As for Alison's dad, he was in the Coast Guard, and like her mom, was rarely home, so Alison felt forced to fend for herself.

Like many of us, Alison inherited both masculine and feminine energy wounds. "I was my own nurturer and protector," she told me with tears in her eyes.

I looked at her gently and said, "Can you see how the need to always be on the go was never wrong? That it was actually you loving yourself? That it was your energetic way of protecting yourself and nurturing yourself, when you didn't receive either from your parents? Your always hustling and being on the go wasn't wrong. It was just coming from wounded energy."

There's nothing wrong with being successful. There's nothing wrong with ambition or being in your masculine energy. It's the masculine that gives us that forward momentum to take the actions necessary to realize our dreams. But when we lean too heavily on it, it causes us to overcompensate and get out of balance.

And so, if you relate to the always-on-the-go, hustling, doing, and acting lifestyle, just ask yourself honestly: Is this energy rooted in the real me? Or is it coming from a wound I haven't yet allowed myself to feel?

Clashing Energies

If you want a quick way to understand where your masculine and feminine energy is out of balance, look at your intimate relationship. If you're single, reflect on past relationships, or even current ones with friends, co-workers, clients, or anywhere you feel resistance, frustration, or emotional charge. What's the energy underneath that dynamic? That's what we're tracking here.

And just to be clear: I'm not saying you "need" to be in a relationship. I spent three years single before I called in my partner, and it was exactly what my soul needed. There are seasons when walking alone is the very medicine our soul needs. And yet, in this world, we're bombarded with messages that something must be wrong if we're not partnered.

Forget all that.

Use whatever's showing up right now as a mirror. When two people come together, there's always an energetic dance just like there is inside of you. Most of the time, one partner leads with masculine energy, the other with feminine. That dynamic is called polarity, and polarity creates flow.

This is what Kia realized. When we started working together, she had a deep mistrust of masculine energy and men. She had been molested as a child by someone at a babysitter's house. Her father was in and out of her life, but mostly absent, so her mom raised her as a single parent, working hard just to keep the family afloat.

When Kia told her mom what had happened, her mom acted fast and protected her by removing her from the situation. Yet the impact had already landed. Like many of us, Kia started searching for love through physical intimacy, unconsciously trying to reclaim something she'd lost. After college, she realized her survival was on her, and that she had to learn how to make money, build a life, and take care of herself.

And she did it!

By the time we met, she was independent, successful, and had a thriving career as a prosecutor. Despite wanting to be in a committed relationship, she found herself still single. She told me the men she was dating seemed nice. They showed up when she needed something, and seemed supportive, yet something felt off.

"I don't know if they're doing these things to appease me," she said, "or if it's who they really are."

As we started to go deeper, talking about the type of men she often dated, what I began to see (and what she started to feel) was that it wasn't really about the men.

It was about her energy.

She was leaning so far into her masculine energy and overcompensating, she was so used to leading, protecting, and doing for herself, that there was no space left for her feminine to breathe. And without that space, there was no room for a partner to show up in their masculine either.

"You're not attracting the man because right now, energetically, you are the man," I told her directly yet softly.

I don't mean this as an identity or as a fault of hers. It was a protective mechanism that had become her default mode. Her masculine was so overdeveloped and overcompensating that her feminine had nowhere to land.

She admitted that she literally didn't know how to rely on or trust men to lead or protect her because she'd never seen it modeled. Not in her home and definitely not in her community. "It was women running everything, because none of the men could be trusted," she admitted.

You see, that's not just a belief. That's an energetic imprint that will dictate the rest of Kia's life, until she decides to go into, heal, and release it. It was a survival pattern born from real pain. But that pattern has kept her locked out of what she truly craves—connection, trust, and the ability to relax into and open her heart.

When you strip it down, Kia didn't know how to surrender, how to receive, or how to be held. She had needed to lead and hold herself for so long that she didn't know how to allow someone to hold her. But deep down that's what she wanted. She wanted to trust, to soften, to come back to her heart and her feminine energy.

What she wanted—what so many of us want—isn't about becoming passive, submissive, and allowing our partners to dominate us. It's simply allowing the feminine to breathe again, balancing it with the strength of our masculine. What Kia actually craved was the ability to move freely between the two energies—giving and receiving, leading and surrendering, protecting and being protected. If Kia could learn to balance the two energies, then she could attract a partner who could do the same.

I encourage you to do the same reflection. Look at your relationships for a moment and ask yourself honestly: *Where am I overcompensating? Where am I shut down? What do I resist? What do I crave? What am I afraid of?*

Whatever energy is imbalanced within you, you will unconsciously seek its opposite in another. Not to complete you. But to show you where the healing is ready to begin.

Constant Fighting

Do you often find yourself always fighting with your partner, parents, friends, co-workers, or kids?

When we're constantly defending or attacking, we're living in our overcompensating masculine. And beneath that—whether we know it or not—is fear. Fear of receiving, learning, growing, and surrendering. Our unconscious mind has boxed us into a limited identity for so long that the only language we know is rejection. The only posture we know is to defend. We've been trained to look for flaws in others, to make them wrong, as it validates the story we learned as children: "People are here to hurt me."

Fighting is a defense mechanism. It's a pattern we learned when we were young. If this hits you, then ask yourself: Did you feel safe? Heard? Seen? Were your thoughts and ideas embraced, or dismissed?

If you're like most people, the answer is no. You've been fighting to be heard, understood, and loved since you were a child. So the person you're fighting with today, be it your spouse, a parent, a friend, is really just the energetic mirror of the one you were fighting back when you were just a kid.

It's the same wound playing out through a different face.

And I'm telling you this so that maybe you'll pause, even just for a breath, and say to yourself, "What if I don't need to fight anymore?"

When I met Aaron and his wife, Abby, they were both so deep in their heads, so reactive, that all they knew was to fight and defend. There was no peace within either of them. No space for love to breathe. They were on guard all the time, just waiting for the next jab, the next argument or disagreement. Just waiting to prove the other wrong and to fight.

They came to a plant medicine ceremony I led, and I remember that one in particular because it was such a profoundly moving journey where, by the end, everyone was hugging each other, crying, and saying "I love you" from a space that felt like home. The energy was pure, sacred, and openhearted. When it ended, Aaron walked up to me and we hugged, and I quietly told him, "Hey, Abby loves you, man."

And the first thing out of his mouth was, "Yeah, bro, go help her. She needs a lot of it."

I pulled back and just looked at him. That moment said everything. After all the depth, all the connection we'd just experienced, he ran right back into the old programming, basically pointed the finger at her. That's how strong the wounded mind is. It will not accept responsibility and will always look to put the ownership elsewhere.

A couple days later, I brought up that moment on a call, and Aaron got a little triggered, which, to me, told me we were right where we needed to be. So I asked him point blank, "What's your default reaction toward Abby?"

To his credit, he paused before explaining that he can see what she does wrong, and he blames her for everything. "She could buy peanut butter at the store, and the first thing I'll say is, 'Why did you buy that kind?'" he shared.

"I'm always in victim consciousness," he went on. The words seemed to stun him even as he admitted them.

"If your first instinct is to blame, then how are you ever going to open your heart to receive love?" I asked him. He got really quiet and had no answer, so I asked him the same question that I ask everyone: "And where do you think you learned that?" I asked.

Without hesitation, he said, "It was one hundred percent from how I was raised. The only way I felt love was by being perfect. If I made a mistake, I got blamed. So I learned to blame others to keep the attention off me."

Feel how deep that is. Can you recognize how much havoc it had been wreaking on Aaron's life? In his relationship with his spouse, and most likely in his other relationships, especially with his kids? Blaming others had become Aaron's shield. A wall that protected him from feeling unworthy or unlovable. And that wall was built through overcompensating masculine energy. But the cost was steep, it came with disconnection from his feminine, from softness, responsibility, and love.

"Blaming others is how the wounded mind avoids accountability," I explained. "It's how it keeps you out of your heart, out of your feminine, and trapped in the illusion that being perfect means being safe. But the deeper that story runs, the more you'll project it onto your partner. You'll keep searching for perfection and punishing anything that falls short. Which means you're doomed."

And then I asked him something else, designed to help him go deeper within himself so he could see his original energetic wounds even more clearly. "How do you think that energy—of blaming, criticizing, pointing out flaws—makes Abby feel?"

This is when his voice softened for the first time. "I know exactly how it feels, because it's how I felt growing up. I felt like I was always being blamed, and I felt ashamed and guilty for not 'getting it right.' And now . . . I'm doing the same thing to her."

That realization cracked something open inside Aaron, because he began quietly crying, releasing the pain that he'd carried, unknowingly, for so long. Finally, I told him he had to tell her. Not just the words, but the energy. "You have to let her feel your heart. Don't come from your mind. Don't perform this. Go into your heart and tell Abby: 'I realize it now. I've been blaming you for everything, and I've never accepted responsibility. I'm sorry.'"

I explained that for real healing to take place, he should only say it when he truly meant it. When his energy was clean, and there were no traces of blame, no attempts to justify his past actions and behaviors. He had to be still in presence, truth, and only in his heart. Because this is how we heal. The wounded mind will fight to keep us from sharing from our vulnerability and truth. It will always try to trick you into hiding and keeping it all in.

But hiding only keeps us trapped and stuck in the old identity, stories, and beliefs. And the moment we speak from our heart, the moment we take responsibility, that's when the story begins unraveling. Healing begins.

Because underneath every defense, every pattern, every argument is a wound and pain. And just past both is our heart and the life, peace, and connection that's waiting for us.

* * *

Remember . . . love has grace.

Whatever's happened in your life, whatever masculine and feminine imbalances you've lived from, please hear this:

You are not broken. You do not need fixing. What you need is *healing.*

When you begin to shine the light on your inner hidden wounds, when you start seeing the connection between your stories, habits, heart, and the energetic imprints and wounds you've lived from, then it might stir up anger, shame, guilt, and other potentially uncomfortable emotions. That's okay. Let the energy rise. Let it stir. That's energy surfacing to be released. That's the frequency leaving your body.

This is the moment of liberation. Freedom doesn't come from pushing harder or doing more. It comes from being whole. It comes from having the courage to leave your mind, go into your heart, open it, and allow the hidden wounds to be brought into the light. It's about honoring both your masculine and feminine, in balance, in harmony, and in truth.

AWAKEN YOU

Discover Your Hidden Energetic Wounds

If you haven't done it yet, go back to the sections describing the three ways our feminine and masculine energy get expressed, and identify the ones that resonated with you, those that triggered a strong visceral reaction or had you pause and go "Wow, that hits."

Underline the descriptions, then one by one, meditate on each for at least two to five minutes, asking, "How does this show up in my life?"

When you're ready, you can take this question deeper, asking, "What happened in my past that caused me to be like this?"

This exercise doesn't have to be done in one sitting. Do it slowly over the course of a week or longer. It's not the pace that matters, it's that you're taking the time to reconnect to your highest self, allowing it to guide you to and through the deep unconscious wounds that have been orchestrating your life.

And here's how to really anchor the awareness: Pick one wound you identified, and write a letter acknowledging it. Speak directly to the part of you that formed in response to that pain. For example on how to begin:

"I see you [fill in the blank]. I understand why you showed up. You were protecting me, keeping me safe, helping me survive . . ."

Let whatever needs to be said come through. When you've completed the letter, read it aloud to yourself while looking in a mirror. Eye to eye. Breath to breath. Feel the energy move through you. And when you're done, place both hands on your heart and say:

"Thank you. I now release you."

This is how we begin releasing and healing those hidden wounds, by witnessing with honesty, with compassion, and with love the energy within and the part of ourselves that created it.

You are not here to bypass your pain. You are here to alchemize it. This is how it starts.

Free Gift: To go deeper, I created a free class to guide you into awareness of how your finances may unknowingly be blocked and limited as a result of unhealed masculine and feminine energy within. To access it, simply go to **dannymorel.com/MFMP**.

CHAPTER 6

LIFE'S MEDICINES

He looks so happy.

It was New Year's Eve, and I was mindlessly scrolling on social media when a friend's post flashed on my phone. This was many years ago, when I had just begun my awakening. I was living alone in a tiny apartment after telling my wife I wanted a divorce. In my heart, I knew it was the right call, yet I can't say that I felt happy or was any closer to understanding what happiness was like. I still felt this numbness and ache in my heart like there was something more for me in life, I just didn't know how to find it.

That's when I caught a friend smiling like I had never seen him before. He was a lot like me. Successful in all the ways that society teaches us to be, yet the vibe he gave me was that maybe he, like me, was living with a feeling of emptiness and unhappiness. To be fully raw and real, we were both dickheads. We both had this arrogance about us back then, as if the world only revolved around us and our desires.

So when I saw him in his social media stories, I was taken aback. He looked like he was glowing from the inside out in a way that I'd never seen from him. I remember thinking, *I know his smile, and that isn't his normal smile*. I had to know his secret. What was he doing, or what had he done, to make him look that happy, because whatever it was, I was going to do it too.

So I texted him immediately and almost instantly got one word back: *ayahuasca*.

I felt a ripple of fear run through my body. Ayahuasca is a psychedelic plant medicine made by brewing different plants from the Amazon into a tea. For thousands of years, shamans have used it in ceremonies and rituals to help heal disease in the mind, body, and spirit. While illegal in the United States, ayahuasca retreats in Mexico and Central and South America have gained popularity with Westerners seeking spiritual awakening and self-help.

For the better part of almost 10 years, I was the guy that judged ayahuasca retreats. People would tell me about "sitting with the medicine" and how incredibly life altering it was. I even noticed drastic changes in them like a new sense of inner peace. Yet I was on such a religious high horse that I would immediately write off ayahuasca as New Age, or the work of the devil, believing it was rooted in witchcraft and that I would go to hell if I ever did any of that stuff. Essentially, I had lived most of my life in a black-and-white world, where only my beliefs were right and any "truth" outside of them were wrong.

Yet I sensed this disconnect rising up within me after my friend's text. I could feel the part of me that wanted to turn away or deny ayahuasca as "devil's work," but there was my buddy, beaming with joy, and a smile I simply couldn't deny.

This was also around the time the pastor had told me that if I got divorced, then I would lose God's favor on my life. So I thought, *If I already lost God's favor, how much worse can things get?* I was questioning everything about life, including what would make me happy and fulfilled.

And so I wondered, *What if they're wrong about ayahuasca too?*

Immediately, I got a strong hit from my intuition to ask my friend for more details, so I did. I was beginning to listen and trust what was coming through me, so when my friend told me about a retreat center in Costa Rica, I looked them up online, and without thinking, hesitating, or second-guessing, I said, "I'm in," and booked a spot in a ceremony a few weeks away.

THE GREAT TESTING

The old me never would have said yes to some spiritual retreat in Costa Rica. I wouldn't have even thought about it—that stuff was in devil's territory, and I was too busy working on my business to "work on myself." Yet I wanted that smile my friend had, and I was willing to try almost *anything* to get it.

Yet I was deeply afraid of what saying yes meant.

When you have strong programming inside that tells you something is "wrong," then it doesn't leave you immediately. I could accept that maybe what my religion taught me wasn't exactly true, but a lot of fears and doubts still lingered. So for weeks, I walked around with this intense doubt, wondering if I was making the right decision.

It was the night before I was set to leave LAX at 6 A.M. when a friend invited me to his place for dinner. I already knew my friend was against this retreat. He had tried talking me out of it, but my mind was set, and I was committed to the experience no matter what came up.

Yet life has a strange way of testing our resolve, especially when we're about to make a decision that could absolutely change our life. I walked into dinner that night at my friend's house, and someone was sitting there . . . a pastor. (Yes, another one.)

It wasn't my old pastor—it was someone I had never met. As soon as we shook hands, I felt something was off. I had started trusting my intuition, so he didn't need to say a word for me to feel something different in his energy. As soon as he started talking, I sensed intense righteousness coming from him. He was one of those people who give off zero kindness or compassion. The type that's filled with judgment.

I had no desire to talk about my trip to Costa Rica the next morning. Yet what we push against tends to come back to us, so, of course, one of the first topics my friend brought up was ayahuasca. He told the pastor all about it. At first, the pastor didn't say a word. He simply stared at me over his plate. I could almost hear all his judgmental thoughts, and I braced myself, preparing for a lecture about walking with the devil.

But what he said hit me harder than any devil talk could.

"People die from that, you know," he finally said rather emotionlessly and in a very casual way, as if stating a fact.

I was already nervous about doing this thing that was so far outside of my norm, but die? I hadn't thought about that. And death was very much on my mind at that time. My mom had died fairly young by today's standards, so I was carrying this intense fear that maybe I would too. I was terrified that cancer might take me like it had her, my friend, and Aunt Jenny, yet I hadn't thought about ayahuasca.

Was I going to Costa Rica to die? Would I leave my boys fatherless? Was this retreat a giant mistake, and was I being warned? The questions zipped through my mind so quickly that I couldn't control them, and I could feel myself starting to sweat and second-guess myself as the energy of fear intensified.

Then just as quickly, something else washed over me. An inner voice that stopped the fear and hit me straight in the heart. *What are you going to do?* I heard within. *Are you going to do what you always do and back down, or are you going to see this through?*

Instantly, something inside of me rose up and said, "F*ck this. I am *all* in."

And just like that, I decided I was going to see it through. I was done. Done listening to people outside of myself who told me what I wanted was right or wrong. I wanted to know the truth about what was blocking me from my authentic smile. What was blocking me from how to actually feel love and happiness, how to find real love with a woman. I wanted to know what needed healing inside of me and what I was meant to do with my life.

Because nothing I had been taught to believe had led me to any of those answers.

I wanted more than to believe—I wanted to *know*. The truth about myself, the truth about God, and the truth about life and what I was here to create.

Most self-help, spiritual, and personal development teachers teach us that the road to change lies in adopting new habits, behaviors, and thoughts. Yes, that's true, and yet for most of us, those changes never stick. We quickly retreat into self-sabotaging behaviors, find ourselves stuck in negative patterns, and continue landing in similar situations with the same type of people again.

Why? Because the *energy* within hasn't changed.

That's the key. To change our lives, we have to change the energy that's driving all of the habits, behaviors, and thoughts. When you change the energy, then those things naturally change as a byproduct of the new energy.

Remember, who you are and the life you are living today was created from the energies that you absorbed as a child. And it has called in the same people, experiences, and circumstances to match. This isn't about blaming yourself. It's not your fault, and you haven't made some terrible mistake. No one has taught you how to release and transmute that energy, so it stays stored and trapped in your body. And this will be the pattern of your life until you reach the point where you say, "Enough. I am done. I am willing to do whatever I have to do to release whatever is blocking me so I can be free."

Free of what? Everything. Free of whatever holds you back. Free of the negative stories, limiting beliefs, and self-sabotaging patterns. Free of the masculine and feminine wounds. Free of the energy of fear, guilt, shame, blame, desire, and more.

Yet for the new you to be born, the old you has to die.

And it's not going to go quietly. That's the scary part, but also it's the part of you that is so powerful. You will call in and attract the moments, the people, the circumstances that will feed that fear and test you one more time to see the level of resolve and courage within.

This is when courage and certainty beyond logic—which we talked about in the Introduction—becomes important. It's an opportunity and a gift, as you get to tap into the courage to go on this journey to change and alter your destiny, forever.

If you are the creator of your life, and you have created whatever it is you don't want in your life, then can you uncreate it?

Yes, yes, you can.

That's how powerful you are. You have the ability to go within and release the energy that no longer serves you so you're free to create from what's been dormant inside of you: the energies of abundance, love, peace, courage, and so much more.

And I'm going to show you how to start that process.

HOW TO RELEASE STORED ENERGY

For most of my life, I experienced heartbreak with women, and I didn't know why. So at an ayahuasca retreat, I brought a picture of myself and a girl named Mimi. She was my very first crush. I was about five years old, and I would follow her around everywhere, wanting her to notice and pay attention to me. I got what I wanted, sort of, only she was really mean-spirited, always picking on me and acting unkind, yet I kept chasing her, and this happened for years.

While Mimi was long gone, the energy of her and my first experience with girls unknowingly remained. I could see the pattern of how all of my relationships had ended in heartbreak, and I wanted that to stop.

As I prepared to go into the ceremony, I set my intention, saying, "Mother Aya, I want to heal the heartbreak that I have with women." And on that journey, she showed me all of these stories of heartbreak with women, and showed me the energy within me that was trapped. The medicine showed me where it all began—with the energy I had picked up from my mother and the heartbreak she received by not having her mother in her life. I realized that what I was experiencing in life was not only a result of my energy, it was far deeper than that. I saw how on my mother's side there was a deep feminine wound that spanned generations upon generations.

I saw how that very energy called in the heartbreak my grandmother received by attracting my grandfather. The heartbreak my mother received by not having her mother present. The heartbreak I received by not having my mother by me during the first two weeks of my life or the fullness of her love available for me as I was growing up. And I was shown how that energy called in Mimi, my first heartbreak, and then the next girl, and the next, and the next.

I saw how absolutely everything that had happened in my life was connected to everyone that came before me. Yes, everything that you've experienced is connected as well. You know what else I saw? That you and I have the ability to be the ones who heal it all. Not just for ourselves, but for our entire ancestral line and all our future generations to come.

That ceremony *blew* my mind. It's why on the third day of our AWAKEN events, we clear any negative energy between you and your ancestral line. Yet even after the deep profound awareness of that ceremony, there was still work to be done.

When my now wife, Jen, showed up in my life, even she fit the pattern. We met on social media and had been DMing each other as friends for two weeks. I saw no signs of a boyfriend, and, honestly, I was in love from the moment I first laid eyes on her. So when she told me she had a boyfriend, I was shocked. Again, more of what I was used to: heartbreak. Yet this felt different; it felt like an opportunity to go deeper within myself and integrate all the lessons I'd received from ceremonies into real life.

I was ready to call in a life partner, and I thought, *If Jen isn't available, I'm going to use this time to cut anything that may be blocking me from the love I want to experience.* For me, that meant more ceremonies, but also more integration. I went through a deep process of solitude. No sex with anyone for six months, a dedication to reconnecting with nature, no TV for over a year, and cord-cutting ceremonies for every partner I had ever been with.

Jen and I had been talking for about three years when she suddenly became single. I knew what I wanted, and it was her. I flew from my home in Texas to London, where she was living, to meet her. On our first date, I was trying so hard to impress her that I wore a double-breasted suit jacket with a pocket square. I had *zero* chill back then. I planned out every detail of our date, down to the exact route we'd walk to the restaurant and the exact timing of everything. I was filled with such anxious energy that she picked up on it, and on my last night in London, she handed me the one thing a guy in love doesn't want to receive . . . the friend card.

I remember thinking there was something seriously off with my masculine energy, and so I sat in ceremony again, and the medicine showed me that for a woman to feel safe with a man, he must be grounded like a tree. It uses nature, as ultimately we are one with nature, and if we pay attention, nature can be one of our greatest teachers. In this case, when the man is the tree, then the woman can be the wind, flowing and free to express her emotions, whatever they may be.

I started to realize that I unknowingly had been creating the heartbreak I received all these years. Most women didn't feel safe with me because I was ungrounded. I tend to get excited when I talk, so I often speak quickly and energetically. Back then, it was like I was on speed. I spoke 10 times faster and often without thinking—a clear sign someone is ungrounded.

I went into the ceremony to clear this, and as I laid there, I felt this pulsing start in the base of my spine. It was this sensation that kept getting bigger and bigger with each breath in, until the pulsing encompassed midway down my thigh and up to my belly button. I had never felt anything like this before, and it made me nervous.

I raised my hand to get the shaman's attention. "Something's wrong, I feel something gushing out of my *culito*," I said, terrified. (That's Spanish slang for "butthole.")

He laughed. "Don't worry, you're just being activated. Enjoy it."

That moment changed my life forever. Because immediately after hearing him say that, I thought, *Wait a minute, you mean to tell me, I spent 43 years of my life not activated?*

That's when another thought struck: *Oh, my God, how many human beings are out there right now who aren't activated?*

Finally, I couldn't help but feel sad for my mom, my tía Jenny, my friend Tony, and all the millions of people who passed away never having had this experience. An experience that I later discovered was my root chakra—an energy center that sits at the base of the spine—opening, and that is what caused me to do this work.

After that experience, I was calmer, more present, and more patient. I became a different version of myself. I couldn't help but think about how many human beings were out there who hadn't been shown this was even possible for them.

Releasing stored energy is a physical experience. There is no book, podcast, or social media post that can cause it. There's no one to hear preach, and no one to believe in. It's you going into you. Accessing the deepest parts of yourself through a spiritual experience (one that I'll invite you to experience at the end of this chapter) and letting go of what's been blocking you all along. That's how you release stored energy, and that's the only way life ever really changes. In truth, it's often a process that happens again and again, each time going deeper and deeper while you're trying different tools and modalities.

Fortunately for us, Source has left us several different "medicines" we can turn to, to help us on this journey.

Meditation

So many of us have hyperactive minds. We're constantly scrolling on our phones, checking e-mail, browsing social media, and texting. We're multitasking, dividing our attention between work, family, friends, visits to the doctor, caring for aging parents, and so much more. It's a constant chattering between what's next, regrets of the past, and multiple distractions, and it's causing our mind to become overloaded. If our mind is always on, then how will we ever be in solitude so we can begin releasing the energy underneath all of those thoughts, actions, emotions, and experiences that make up the pattern of our days?

The answer is meditation. We get to make the time and space in our lives to quiet our mind and be one with ourselves. Meditation stills the mind, and when the mind is still enough for long enough, it can even lead us into a deep and profound spiritual experience. Though, I will say, having that profound of an experience from just meditating isn't easy. For most of us, including myself when I began, our minds are so hyperactive and we're so disconnected from our hearts that it might require a deeper practice.

Yet there are three meditations that I like to teach. When you're starting out, even beginning with three minutes can make a big impact, and you can increase the time as you feel comfortable.

From the list below, choose one meditation to try first, and focus on taking three slow breaths in, and exhaling for three slow breaths out, then begin.

Meditation #1: Focus on your breath

The easiest way to meditate is simply to focus all of your energy and awareness on your breath. It's called *conscious breathing*. Think about that for a second: The thing that keeps us alive we do unconsciously.

If it is so powerful that it keeps us alive, imagine how much more potent it can be if we do it consciously?

In and out, in and out. That's it. No thoughts of what you have to do later or what happened yesterday. All your attention gets placed on what's going in and what's going out and the impact and sensations it's providing on your body.

As you do this, thoughts will come up. Just notice them like clouds passing in the sky and continue to breathe, focusing your attention on the inhale and exhale. This is a practice in disconnecting from the energy of these thoughts, so the more they come up, the more you become comfortable allowing them to pass through your mind and body.

Because, yes, thoughts are energy too, and when we hold on to the same thoughts, they too get stored.

Meditation #2: Focus on the space within you

The second easiest way to meditate if you're just starting is to focus all your awareness on the space within you. Just close your eyes and picture the outline of your body. Now, focus all of your attention on the space within your shape. This is a game changer, and it creates stillness and peace within you.

When you give yourself the task of focusing on the space within, the mind can't be hyperactive. And as you do that, you often can access the most powerful of practices: the present moment. There's no worrying about the future or thinking about the past. It all falls away as you're still and in presence, which is all there ever is.

Meditation #3: Focus on the space outside of you

Now, to take this a step further, remember the outline of your body? Now visualize it going away and that space within you becoming one with the space outside of you.

This is the expansiveness of space, not the room or the house you're in, but everything outside of you. What you will feel eventually, is that your mind is going to try to hold on to the body, or the concept of the body. And the more you practice, the closer you'll get to that magical moment you become one with everything. And everything you once thought was important—time, space, even your identity—will slowly disappear. *That* is a magical moment. You might even shed a tear when you finally experience it.

Breathwork

I've studied meditation and attended many popular retreats hosted by some of the biggest names in the industry. I love it, and it's possible to go on a deep journey within you to release the energy while having a profound spiritual experience.

I've also been in the room where it seems the people onstage are having this incredible, transcendental journey, yet everyone else, myself included, not so much. I've lost count of how many retreats I've gone to where fellow attendees tell me they felt nothing and experienced nothing.

That's because to go so deep into a meditation that you can release the trapped energy takes a lot of work and practice. As I just mentioned, our minds are too active, and they don't want us to let go. Remember, the wounded mind wants to keep us safe, and safe means predictable. It doesn't want us to let go, because in its wounded state, it mistakenly believes we're safe. Returning to our hearts is where the original wound was, and so our minds will do everything and anything to keep us out.

That makes meditation on its own really tough for most of us, and it's why I teach it with breathwork. The breath takes us out of our minds and centers us in our body. I started in-person events because I wanted everyone to experience the profound energetic release and spiritual experience that I had using ayahuasca, but without them having to go on a plant-medicine journey. I'm a huge proponent of using plant medicines, yet, I know for various reasons, it's not for everyone and isn't easily accessible. Ayahuasca, for example, is illegal in the United States. You have to leave the country and find a reputable, trustworthy retreat center, which isn't possible for everyone.

With breathwork there are no restrictions and nothing exterior needed. It's simply you breathing in a structured, patterned way for a set period of time. When you do it correctly and with intention, you can have as deep and as profound a spiritual journey as you would with plant medicine. I've seen absolute mind-blowing miracles happen at our online events and at our three-day, in-person event, Awaken Your Highest Self. Each event has a breathwork practice, yes, even the virtual ones.

I've seen people heal lifetime issues with their bodies, discover the root cause of their limiting beliefs, and even connect with their highest self, spirit guides, ancestors, and angels, and release long-held energy that's been stored in their body.

At the end of this chapter, I'm going to invite you to experience breathwork with me from the comfort of your own home.

Yoga

Yoga is one of the most powerful tools you can use to release stored energy, because it reconnects you to your mind, body, and heart. Our bodies hold on to the energy of our experiences until we release them. So the tight hips, chronic pain in the neck, and sore shoulders that you can't seem to work out are actually your body showing you that there's resistance within you that needs to be shed.

In my work with people using past-life regression techniques, I've found it fascinating how often some of what is stored in the body relates to unhealed trauma from previous lives. Remember, you're a soul having a human experience, and sometimes that soul has come here to work through some unfinished business.

One of the reasons why I love yoga so much is because it gets your body moving, flowing, and breathing. The magic comes when you get in complete flow, when body, breath, and movement become one. Once you stop and go into savasana (corpse pose), you can actually have a spiritual experience as a result.

I've had experiences where after a yoga session, I'll lie in savasana and get visions, messages delivered, and can feel some of the stored energy release. That's because the body, mind, and breath are working together, then you're opened, and boom! It's peaceful and beautiful, and you can release and receive.

Grounding

When I moved to Austin in 2022, I decided to not have a television. "What are you going to do with your kids?" a friend wondered. They seemed shocked by the idea, but I didn't want the distraction of media, entertainment, or even sports around me. Matter of fact, the more I journeyed within, the more it felt like all of it was actually designed to keep me in a constant state of distraction.

So I disconnected from the box I was being put in and started going on walks and spending time in nature. It was like I traveled back in time. I was doing activities and living life in the way they did in the early 1900s and farther back. At first, it was strange, but gradually, I began relishing the time spent outdoors. I found thoughts, emotions, and even memories coming to the surface as I walked and sat outside. That's when I realized I could even ask Mother Nature to help me clear energy. I could actually give the energy to her and allow her healing touch to nourish and restore me in return.

In the book *Jesus and the Essenes*, it's said that one of Jesus's lost teachings was that if you want to heal your life, then let the wind, sun, fire, and ground heal you, because Mother Earth is the greatest healer of all.

We live during a time in history when humans are so disconnected from Mother Earth that we don't ever give her the opportunity to heal us. Have you ever wondered why, when you go on vacation and lie out in the sun, walk on the beach, spend time in a forest, or swim in a lake or ocean you feel renewed, energized, and happy after?

It's because you're one with Mother Nature, and she's healing you on an energetic level.

Reconnecting with Mother Nature is vital for our overall well-being. It restores our intrinsic bond with the earth, which is essential for maintaining balance in our lives. On an energetic level, nature helps us ground ourselves, dispelling the chaotic energy of modern life and harmonizing our internal rhythms with the natural world. This grounding effect stabilizes our emotions and fosters a deep sense of calm and centeredness.

Spending time in nature has profound physical and mental benefits. Studies show that it can reduce stress, and lower anxiety and depression,[2] reduce blood pressure, improve immune function, and enhance mental clarity.[3] I'd argue those benefits are the result of releasing the trapped energy, moving the negative, fear-based, low-frequency energies out and making space for the others.

Connecting with Mother Earth is also a reconnection to ourselves, as we aren't separate from nature; we are part of it. Just as the earth cycles through seasons, growth, and renewal, so do we. By attuning ourselves to these natural rhythms, we reconnect with the cycles of our own lives, fostering self-awareness and inner peace. This deep connection reminds us of our place within the larger web of life, helping us to feel more grounded, whole, and in tune with our true nature.

In this way, connecting with the earth is a powerful act of self-care and spiritual nourishment, aligning us with the essence of who we are at our core.

All you have to do is go outside, take off your socks and shoes, feel the ground beneath your feet, and allow whatever energy is inside of you to be released through your soles into the ground. This is a practice called grounding, or earthing. It helps to align your body's energetic frequency.

It's a simple practice. Stand with your feet connected to the earth. Hold your hands out to your side and stand proud and tall like a thousand-year-old tree. Feel yourself rooted deeply, and visualize roots coming from the bottom of your feet, connecting into the core of the earth.

Visualize a golden light coming from the center of the earth, up through those roots, into your feet, then pouring through all your limbs, sexual organs, stomach, chest, heart, throat, and all the way to the top of your head. Visualize this energy cleansing and clearing whatever stuck and stored energy is trapped inside of you. Feel that energy melt away as the golden light floods your entire being.

Stand like this for 10 minutes or more three times a week, or whenever you feel anxiety or high levels of stress.

Mirror Work

Mirror work is a powerful tool for reconnecting with our hearts, and it can begin the journey of loving and knowing ourselves in a much deeper way. It begins by standing or sitting in front of a mirror for three minutes. All you're going to do is stare straight into your eyes. Make it intimate. Make it special.

Try not to look away. I get that it's probably going to feel tough, especially at first. Your initial instinct will be to avoid your gaze, because you want to avoid yourself, which is avoiding your power. Yet this is how we start letting go. Looking ourselves in the eye creates space for honesty and vulnerability where we can express pride, forgiveness, and commitment directly to ourselves.

This is a practice in rebuilding the relationship we have with ourselves. We replace the one from fear and separation to create one rooted in self-love and acceptance.

Mirror work has three components. For each statement, you'll say three different things, three times.

1. "I am proud of myself for ______________."

For many of us, society, religion, even our families teach us to downplay our talents, skills, and achievements. This keeps us stuck in the energies of judgment, disempowerment, and shyness. When we look ourselves in the eyes and say what we're proud of ourselves for, it releases the negative energies and activates ones like empowerment and confidence.

2. "I forgive myself for ______________."

This exercise allows you to release the energies of guilt, shame, and self-blame that may be holding you back.

3. "I am committed to ______________."

This affirms your intention to grow, heal, and move forward.

Mirror work is about owning our limiting stories and our willingness to create new ones. It's about making peace within ourselves for the past and present, for the energies we unknowingly absorbed and that have been creating our lives, and our commitment to letting them go so we can make space for new energy, and new life, to be born.

Try using this medicine once a day for 30 days and see what happens.

Cord-Cutting

Finally, cord-cutting is a powerful tool for releasing energetic ties that bind you to past relationships and experiences. These energetic cords, often formed through intense emotional connections, can keep you tethered to old wounds, draining your energy and preventing you from moving forward. By consciously cutting these cords, you free yourself from the lingering emotional attachments that no longer serve you, creating space for healing and renewal.

Before I met my wife, Jen, I got a clear download (a message from above) that I was to cut cords with anyone I had ever been intimate with. Physical intimacy with someone creates an energetic tie with them. A soul tie. It keeps you connected with your past intimate partners' energies and even their fears.

For example, when we're with someone intimately, we exchange energy sexually, which creates a cord, connecting us energetically with our partners. So we can be in another relationship and life is great, yet the energy of our ex can still linger and show up in our new relationship. Our relationship with our new partner might be completely different than our last, yet we respond, behave, and act in similar ways that we did with our previous one. That's because we still carry the energy of that partner and relationship within us.

Cord-cutting is not about severing all connections with people from your past. It's about releasing the low-frequency energies that have accumulated over time. This practice even helps to cut ties with the energy you have with your parents, your current relationship, your children, and even, when you're ready, your old self.

If you want to try cord-cutting, sit in a meditative position and take a few deep breaths in and out, allowing your voice to be heard through an "ahhh" on the exhale. Be in the moment. Let go of the need to know how long this will take, where this journey is going, or where it will take you.

Notice if your mind starts to immediately become overactive, thinking about everything you need to do, what happened yesterday, or how this practice won't work. Just tell your mind, "Everything is okay. I'm in charge now."

Know you are safe. Know you are loved. Know you are held. Now, I want you to call in the person whose energy you're releasing. To be clear, you're ready to let go of the attachment to the pain and the energy that was exchanged and imprinted on you, however long ago it happened. I want you to see them, and then envision a light within them and surrounding their body—that's their soul standing in front of you.

Look at their heart, and I want you to see a cord of white energy connecting their heart to yours. Feel this cord of energy, what it has done to your body and life, and prepare yourself to let go. Next, we're going to use the Ho'oponopono prayer, an ancient Hawaiian practice, to clear the energy.

In the silence of your heart, state the words, "I'm sorry."

This apology can be to the other person and to you. Maybe to yourself, you're apologizing for whatever comes up that you feel you didn't do for yourself, whether that's speaking your truth, standing up for yourself, honoring yourself, staying in the relationship, whatever it is. And to the other person, maybe you weren't in your strength, honesty, truth, or integrity. Maybe you mistreated them. Let's clear that energy right now.

Second, tell the person in front of you, "Please forgive me."

What do you need to forgive in both them and yourself? What do you forgive that they did or were to you? What do you forgive that you did or weren't to yourself or them?

Third, say, "Thank you."

For if we allow it, in the midst of any pain we can find both a lesson and a gift. Thank them for the good times, and thank yourself for whatever comes up.

And finally, send them off with love by saying the words, "I love you."

Remember this takes courage, yet when we want more love in our lives, we must first begin to see everything through the eyes of love, and that includes pain. As in the midst of everything, that person was simply a reflection of a deep part of you that was unseen or unhealed. So send them your love from your heart, and then give yourself that same energy.

Now take your right hand, which is your masculine hand, and with your index and middle finger make the form of scissors and place them over the cord. And when you're ready to decide to release that which no longer serves you, cut the cord.

A SACRED JOURNEY INTO PLANT AND MUSHROOM MEDICINE

It's interesting to me how so many things that society and religion have told us are "bad" or labeled as "drugs" are actually some of the very things that help us to awaken, heal, and transform our lives. Nowhere have I seen this more than with plant medicines, particularly ayahuasca, mushrooms, and cannabis.

Can these substances be abused and create harm for us? Well, that depends on us. We create everything, yes, even our experiences with the plants. When our intentions aren't grounded in healing, and we approach them with disrespect and dishonor, then, yes, we're going to receive an experience that matches our intention. Once we get past our own negative beliefs about them, we discover the truth: that the plants are here to help us heal. For thousands of years, cultures all over the globe have worked with plant and mushroom medicines to help people to heal physically, emotionally, mentally, and spiritually.

In my eyes, not only do these plant-based medicines come from Mother Nature, but God purposely put them here for us to use when we are ready to awaken and heal.

I love and have used all of the non-plant and mushroom modalities that we already mentioned in this chapter. Yet, if you ask me to pick the top medicine, I'd choose plants and mushrooms, particularly ayahuasca, cannabis, and mushrooms because they allow us to tap into our highest self, connecting on a spiritual level in a way that's easier for us to accept and access.

Is it possible to have profound spiritual experiences using the other modalities? Absolutely, and yet we've lived disconnected from our hearts as a society for so long. Living in a world largely ruled by the mind and fear. So I believe we need the plants, at this particular moment in time, to help us connect to all the healing that's available to us. Healing that our mind will constantly fight to keep us from.

Plant and mushroom medicines place us squarely in the intuitive, spiritual realm that defies all logic and reason, but leave us knowing and sensing on a deep level that something has changed, something is different about us, something has been left behind when the experience is finished. For many of us, it's just too difficult to tap into our highest self, hearing, feeling, and sensing the energy of love, God, and oneness on our own.

That's not because of a human condition or failure on our part. It's because as human beings, thousands of years ago, we lived without phones, televisions, buildings, processed foods, chemicals, and all the toxins in our environment. The energy of today has our soul locked up inside our bodies. It's like layer after layer of energy that we have to sift through before we can get through to our hearts and highest selves. For a lot of us, myself included, there are simply too many layers.

That's where plant and mushroom medicine can come in. They help us to unlock ourselves and bypass all the stuff clinging to us from modern life.

Sitting in Ceremony

I've mentioned "sitting in ceremony" a lot, so what is it? It's the difference between using and abusing the plant medicine for recreational purposes versus sitting with the medicine in a ceremonial, sacred way to elicit healing and transformation.

When we sit with the medicine, it has to be with guidance, under care of a professional, and under sacred ceremony filled with intention. Because the medicine will literally meet you at your intention. The same way the medicine showed me my patterns and wounds with my mother and father is the same way it will meet you at all of your blockages in life.

That's why you need to be in a safe space, with people you trust, with guides you trust, and who are reliable. If you're alone, or with people using these medicines to "party," or with people who don't have experience to help guide you, then don't do it all.

While I believe everyone can benefit from plant medicine, I also recognize it's not right for everybody for various reasons and at different times in their lives. Nor is it a substitute for medical attention or advice.

There can be a dark side to using plant medicine. It's not that the plants are dark, it's the energy being brought to how they are used, the inexperience of some "shamans" and "medicine men and women" who are leading others, and their darker intentions. I've seen retreat centers and "healers" use plant medicine in ways that don't honor how sacred and beautiful these medicines really are.

And as more people, especially in the West, are drawn to the plants and mushrooms, more sacred medicine spaces have become commercialized. If you choose to work with plant medicine, please make sure the retreat center is safe, respectful, and committed to supporting you through the deep integration work that's necessary after the ceremony is over.

CHOOSE YOUR OWN ADVENTURE

When I started my journey, I went all in. Yet in truth, I'm just wired like that . . . a little crazy in that way. I encourage you to take your time and feel into what feels like the best path for you. There are so many other ways to heal that I haven't mentioned, that may fit better for you. Maybe that's acupuncture, sound healing, massage, reiki, qigong, tai chi, eye movement desensitization and reprocessing (known as EMDR), or emotional freedom technique (known as EFT).

This is a practice in reconnecting with your highest self, so I don't even want you to take my word on any of this. Take your own.

LIFE IS MEDICINE

Jen and I were dating when she told me she didn't think I was her dream guy. I sat back in my chair, put my arms over my head, and said, "That's cool, but you're never going to find anyone like me anyway."

I couldn't believe she said that to me, and my response came from classic wounded energy. Yet when I got quiet with myself, I realized it was Source bringing me face-to-face with the critical and surface-level parts of myself that had been programmed by fear. That one line showed me the energy of abandonment, shame, loneliness, and fear. All energies that I thought had long ago left my body. They hadn't. Because if there were no wounds left, and no energy of fear trapped inside of me, I would have watched what she said pass by me like a bird in flight. Actually, she probably never would have said those words in the first place.

We cannot feel hurt unless there is something inside of us already hurting.

The most transformative moment actually comes when we realize that whatever hurts or wounds us now is simply life showing us exactly what energy remains trapped inside. It's showing us what needs releasing and healing in order for us to be whole and in oneness once again.

When you allow yourself to really go into these healing modalities and start the process of releasing and freeing the energies of grief, shame, guilt, blame, sadness, and fear from your body, you will feel emotional pain. The modalities aren't shortcuts. There is no such thing. You will come face-to-face with the energies that have caused your deep woundings.

You see this clearly when you use any healing modality or sit in ceremony. Yet what you learn as you keep sitting in ceremony, keep committing to releasing and healing the energy within, is that very quickly, if you can allow this, all of life becomes the ceremony.

Life becomes medicine.

All of life is medicine.

Because everyone and everything exists to teach and help you heal, you can return to your heart.

Right now, are you scared to try one or more of these medicines? It's okay to feel this way. Now watch this.

Could it be that your relationship to the medicine is your relationship to life?

Could it be that the same way that you're scared to sit with the medicine is the same way that you're scared to sit with yourself?

Could it be that the same way you're scared to sit with the medicine is the same way you're scared to go out and start a business?

Could it be that the same way you're scared to sit with the medicine is the same way you're scared to go all in when you're uncomfortable?

Could it be that the same way you're scared to sit with the medicine is the same way that you're scared to travel and be free?

Could it be that the same way you're scared to sit with the medicine is the same way that you're scared to risk and grow, to be seen and to be heard?

Let me tell you the answers to each of those questions. It's *yes*.

Whatever medicine you choose will simply reflect your life and energy within. It will show you where you are—revealing your deepest insecurities, fears, and the energy that you're living from. So, yes, it's going to feel scary at first, because that energy doesn't want to die, and releasing it will lead to a new you.

And, yes, it's also so beautiful because the scarier it is, the more that is waiting for you on the other side.

Is food beautiful and healing? Yes or no? Has food been used to create illness and disease? Yes or no?

Are relationships beautiful and healing? Yes or no? Have relationships been created to cause heartbreak and pain? Yes or no?

So could life be beautiful and healing? Yes or no?

All of life can either be a poison or medicine, the choice is yours. And what you choose will direct the course of your life from this day forward.

AWAKEN YOU
Integrate the Medicines

It would be my absolute honor to lead you through a beautiful and profound spiritual experience through my guided breathwork. Thousands have flown in from all over the world to experience it, and I'd love to give you access to it absolutely free. To access it, simply go to **dannymorel.com/freebreathwork**.

CHAPTER 7

THE POWER OF FORGIVENESS

There are moments when everything in life changes. One of those was when I stood onstage, leading about 800 people through a profound breathwork experience at AWAKEN. Scanning the audience, I noticed so many people crying, their bodies shaking and trembling, as they likely were releasing lifetimes' worth of trapped energy. I could see their breakthroughs in real time, watching them self-actualize before my eyes.

What did I do to deserve this?

I felt so humbled that people would place their trust in me to guide them through their awakening process. *How lucky am I that I get to wake up every day, helping people heal and transform their lives?* I felt the energy of gratitude, peace, and love wash through me.

And as I stood there in awe and feeling such gratefulness for life, I heard God clearly speak to me.

"You will never help them be all they are intended to become if you don't heal yourself fully and become all you're intended to become."

Immediately, my crazy-ass ego tossed back, *"What do you mean? I am all that I can become. Look at this? Who else is doing breathwork with this size of an audience?"*

As soon as I said that, God bounced back.

"Yes, and you still have to forgive your dad."

Despite all the healing I had done, you would have thought that I would have responded with a little peace, understanding, and acceptance. Not a chance. I immediately ran back into anger, judgment, and unforgiveness.

"Nope. Not doing that," I shot back. *"You don't know what he did to me or my brothers. You don't know how he left me, mistreated me, how he wasn't there when I needed him most."*

Obviously, it wasn't God who didn't know.

It was me.

I didn't know that I was still holding on to so much unresolved resentment toward my father and my past. So I didn't want to forgive him or even think about him for that matter. I had placed him in a box and left him there, avoiding the pain he'd caused me and my brothers.

Yet I'd done enough of this work to know what would have to happen. I knew I could choose to either hold on or let go. I knew the outcomes both would have on my life, and I knew holding on simply wasn't an option for me any longer in any area of my life.

Eventually, I'd have to forgive him if I ever wanted to fully return to my heart.

WHY FORGIVENESS

The healing process intensifies with your parents, because that's where everything began.

They're where you learned about life. They're who you depended on for your survival. Maybe they were the first place you felt pain, rejection, or confusion—all of what feels so common today. They were what you depended on for your survival. They were who you first downloaded codes about life from.

Take a deep breath, because here's where things will get uncomfortable and yet profoundly freeing.

The resistance and unforgiveness that you have toward your father is the resistance and unforgiveness that you have toward your masculine energy. Toward the masculine part of yourself, and to the masculine energy of Source, or God.

And the resistance and unforgiveness that you have toward your mother is the resistance and unforgiveness you have toward your own feminine energy. Toward the feminine part of yourself, and to the feminine energy of Source, or God.

And both of these are the cause of the blockages in your life—of absolutely *everything* in your life. From the money you earn or don't earn to the partners you attract or don't attract, the relationships you're in or not, even your health. All of it can be linked back to your relationship with your mother and father, because any negative energy you have toward those people who gave you the gift of life is essentially a negative energy you carry toward life itself.

I know this is deep, and through the work I do with people, I've become fully aware of just how damaging our parents can be, so let's take this slowly and work through it together.

In my journey, I became aware (step one) of just how much the unforgiveness I had within me was blocking me from everything I wanted to become.

You see, when we carry negative energy toward our father, our masculine is impacted. This creates blockages around our ability to envision the future, to make and execute plans, and to have the discipline to put them into action.

When we carry negative energy toward our mother, our feminine is impacted, which can lead to blockages around allowing ourselves to fully receive from life versus going out, grinding, "making it happen," and "effort-ing" our way through the world.

The energy of unforgiveness, resentment, comparison, maybe fear our parents taught us, confusion . . . all of it is very low-vibrational energy. The very energy blocking you from creating and receiving a life of abundance, freedom, and fulfillment. Because when you live from low vibration in one area of your life, you live from it in all areas.

Remember the same way you learned and absorbed these energies is the same way you can unlearn and release them.

HEALING THE HEART

Allowing the energy of forgiveness into our lives isn't about condoning or rationalizing what happened to us, our parents' behaviors, or in extreme cases, excusing horrific abuse. It's about freeing ourselves from the *energy* of everything we experienced so we can heal the wounds to *our* masculine and feminine and return to oneness within.

So it's not actually about our parents; it's about us.

So how do you start activating the energy of forgiveness toward your parents?

Ask and It Will Be Given

It begins with a decision and a request for help. You don't have to take any steps other than to simply be open to letting go. One of the ways in which you can open yourself is to simply speak it into existence.

Say into the center of your being:

> *"Source [God or whatever you want to call it], I am ready to let go of the pain I've been harboring toward my parents. Bring to me the exact circumstances, people, occurrences, and guiding I need to fully release any and all negative energy toward the two people who gave me my life. I am ready to open myself to healing and your guidance. Please show me the path, make it clear, and I will follow it."*

Once you speak something like this into existence, just be patient with yourself while also becoming aware of what starts showing up for you.

Real healing is supernatural, and when it comes to forgiving our mother and father, we are going to need help from the Divine. Maybe, just maybe, it's time for you to pause and go do that breathwork I offered you at the end of the last chapter.

The Willingness to Let Go, Surrender, and Feel Compassion

Next comes willingness—the willingness to give yourself space within to forgive, to let go, even just a little, of parts of the pain, fear, and anger you've held on to that's connected to your parents.

Here are some questions to help you through this process:

- What if your parents were the way they were with you as a perfect part of your life's journey and soul's evolution?
- What if your parents were the way they were with you because their parents were the way they were with them?
- What if the pain that they passed on to you was the exact same pain that was passed on to them?
- What if your parents mistreated you, didn't love you the way you needed or wanted, or even abused you because their parents mistreated them, didn't love them the way they needed or wanted, or even abused them?

I know this is deep, so please be gentle with yourself and take a few deep breaths as you ponder these tough questions. Feel what you're feeling, and know that it's okay. You don't have to race through whatever comes up. Just try breathing through the sensation, focusing on your breath and the inhales and exhales. Notice what you feel and if there's any sensation in your body like a tightness in your neck or shoulder, your hands burning.

Whatever is coming up for you, remind yourself: *It's just energy.*

And you can visualize that energy moving through your body too. See in your mind's eye where it is, then move it down to the soles of your feet or up to the crown of your head, and on an exhale, breathe it out into the love and light of the Universe, returning it to Source, to Creator, to God.

Wherever you are, and whatever you're experiencing, I am right there with you. I've been through this. I know it's tough. For some of us, we may have no recollection of the wounding, just a vague sense that something is off inside. For others, the memories and our feelings toward our parents are right there.

With these questions, you have begun the process of moving from victim to creator consciousness. It's beginning to separate yourself from the belief that "it's my parents' fault," which is why you can't forgive. It's beginning to bring you out of the 3D and into the 5D world, from societal into spiritual.

It's beginning to open you to the *possibility* that maybe the experiences you had as a child were actually a part of your soul's path, and in doing so, you move out of resistance and into acceptance.

What if you stepped into the possibility that your soul is actually here on a journey to transcend all the pain that you've experienced so you can return to your heart, highest self, and oneness with the Creator?

What if the pain you experienced as a child is what actually allows you to access the freedom you're searching for?

What if your parents were exactly and perfectly the way you needed them to be so you could find the deepest, most powerful forgiveness a human being can have, which is forgiving their mother and father?

And what if that's the very thing you do, just by choosing to see that the only way a parent can ever provide a child with pain is if there's pain living inside of them?

Sit with that for a moment.

The only way a parent, or any human for that matter, can cause pain in another is if that pain was caused to them.

And where did that pain come from?

I can guarantee you, if you look closely at the energy underneath your mother's and/or father's actions, words, and what went unspoken, it was the same energy they experienced from their parents or caretakers. The same sadness, hurt, or disappointment that you may have felt as a little boy or girl was exactly the same as what they felt as a little boy or girl. Just as you were once a blank slate, your parents were too. As were your grandparents and great-grandparents and so on down through your ancestors.

Pause again. Take a deep breath and just feel what's coming up, knowing that whatever it is, it's okay. Again, whatever you're feeling, wherever you are, I'm right there with you, I've gone through this exact process and awakening.

We openly step into forgiveness when we can see that the pain in us was also the pain in our parents.

We enter the energy of forgiveness when we can see that the pain in us was also the pain in our parents.

That one day long ago, they too were an innocent little boy or girl just like us. And just like us, they were a child looking for only one thing: *love*. They, too, were once a child who didn't receive love the way they needed or wanted, and they were left brokenhearted and in tears. Just like you.

Can you feel that? In your body?

That's God, the Divine, the Creator, the Source of everything and love. Feel it. Let that energy move. Let your body release it.

Forgiveness is allowing yourself to let go of every story, belief, and thought—to realize that what your unconscious, wounded mind said was wrong. When you can see the wounded child in your mom and dad, and have compassion for that little boy and girl who didn't receive love, who felt everything that you feel.

Life changes forever in this beautiful moment. And the truth is there's not much to "do"—all that's required is for you to simply "allow." Allow your mind and heart to see and feel what it must have felt like for them to feel what they felt as children.

Whatever you experienced from your parents, you never deserved. You deserved love, safety, nurturing, comfort, support, and more. I'm sorry you may have received the opposite. I honor your experience.

Now, take a moment to close your eyes, and place your right hand on your belly, and your left hand over your heart. Connect to the child within you. Not just as the man or woman who remembers, but the little intuitive, energetic being who experienced the initial wounding, which you may not even remember. It could just be a feeling stored in your body. Whatever it is, send love and compassion to him or her. Feel their heart break, what they had to navigate and find a way to survive, and how it informed their little mind. Have compassion for how you didn't know any better when you created the limiting stories and beliefs. All you were trying to do was to stay out of your heart, where the pain was too much to bear.

Let the child within know that it did nothing wrong. Offer love and compassion to that little boy or little girl who is still a part of you.

This is the sacred rite of forgiveness—of our little self and our parents.

This is love.

Letting go.

Surrender.

Compassion.

All of it, if and when you're ready, leads to one place: forgiveness.

THE GIFT IN PAIN

Life can open in miraculous ways when you become willing to allow the sacred act of forgiveness a place in your heart. This is why I say there's nothing we have to do. This isn't a physical act we take. It's simply a process of allowing ourselves to let go of what we now know no longer serves us.

I know it's hard. I also know there's a part of you that doesn't want to let go. I know because that's the same part of me that didn't want to forgive my dad. Take your time with it all, just tell God that you're willing and allow it all to take shape exactly as it's intended to unfold. If you can allow into your consciousness and heart, even for a few minutes, some compassion for your parents as they were as little boys or girls, then it will begin changing you in profound ways.

I wept for days when I realized that everything my father wasn't for me was because his father wasn't for him. No one was a dad to him. And I saw him as a little boy who had no direction, guidance, or love from his father. When I finally allowed myself to see that, and to feel what it must have felt like for him as a little boy, disowned by his father, I felt my heart break. And with it, all hell broke loose. All hell, all darkness that lived within me, started to slowly fall away.

I pictured what it must have felt like for my dad to feel all alone. My grandmother shipping him off to New York City to live with strangers for most of his childhood. And I thought, *What must he have felt at night in bed, wondering who his father was, wondering when his mother would love him enough to let him come home?*

When I was able to finally connect to my father's little self, that's when I was able to start forgiving him. I mourned for him, because I realized the pain he passed on to me was only the pain that was once given to him. And I mourned for myself, for the little boy who just wanted his father's love, guidance, attention, and direction.

You see, my father abandoned me because he was abandoned. He never had a father, so how could I expect him to give me what he never received?

When I realized this, I knew I had to make a decision. I could either live the rest of my life carrying the energies of anger, resentment, and blame on my back, or I could say, "I don't know how I'm going to do this, I don't know how long it will take, but I'm ready to start letting go of all this energy I've carried with me my entire life." All you need is the willingness to let go; God will meet you at the willingness and make the pathway to healing clear.

When you step away and accept your parents were once little boys and girls who also never received love and what they needed from their parents, it allows you the space to begin accepting who they are, and why they treated you the way they did.

The space to feel compassion for them.

And maybe after compassion, a little forgiveness.

And after forgiveness, what naturally follows is release. A release of the energy you've held on to.

And after releasing and letting go of that energy, the process of healing your own life amplifies.

Because the compassion you feel for them is the compassion you get to feel for yourself. Compassion for the little boy or girl who just wanted to be loved and accepted, and who, deep down, still yearns for that.

If you can learn to have acceptance and compassion for your mom and dad, then you can learn to have acceptance and compassion for yourself and life. This is when your life can truly begin to transform. Because ultimately, you're not separate from your mom and dad. You are them, and they are you.

I've been fortunate to help thousands of people work through this process, and I've witnessed seemingly miraculous transformations. People whose stories and childhoods have contained horrific abuse and trauma, which some people might call unforgivable.

Forgiveness is a journey. It's not something that happens immediately. It takes time for the heart to feel safe and reopen. For context, it took me a good year and a half to really feel forgiveness and love in my heart for my father.

And why do we forgive? Not to condone or excuse what happened to us or bypass those feelings. We forgive to set ourselves free. To remove the distortions and blockages in our hearts, and reveal our true, authentic selves.

You cannot change your life from the present. You are who you are today because of the past. So to change, you go into the past, learn to accept it, forgive those who hurt you, find a gift in it all, and then let go.

If you allow yourself to see it, there's a gift in the pain you have experienced with your parents. From what I've seen, the deeper the pain, the deeper the gift that's available.

The greatest gift my father gave to me was acceptance. From him, I learned that everything in life is perfect. Everything we experience is designed to lead us to the moment when we can wake up, choose to heal, and transform our lives.

This wasn't revealed to me at first. It wasn't until I met with my father in the Dominican Republic after reconnecting. I was going through the process of forgiving him when he called me out of the blue for my birthday one year. We slowly started talking more, and when I saw him in person, I found his truth. He told me how he had tried to work things out with my mother, and how he never wanted her to move me and my brothers to California. But it was what she wanted. As he explained it, he felt he had no choice but to let us go.

As he was sharing his story with me, it felt like I was hearing myself describe my relationship with my ex-wife. Like my mother, my ex told me she was moving to Austin with my boys, and I faced the same fork-in-the-road moment my father had. Instead of letting my boys go, I moved to Texas. Without my father deciding to not follow us, I may have never decided to follow my kids. That was my gift: The pain showed me how much I valued being there for my kids.

YOU GET TO CHOOSE

You don't have to forgive . . . you get to.

You don't have to forgive . . .
you get to.

This is the deliciousness of life. This is why there are so many souls above us right now waiting to come to Earth. For the opportunity to feel. For the opportunity to release. For the opportunity to transcend.

You get to experience pain. You get to experience anger. You get to experience hurt, and on the flip side, you get to experience compassion. And you get to experience surrender of that pain, and through all of it, yes, you get to experience the beauty of forgiveness.

Again, you don't have to. You *get* to.

Just a question to ponder from my heart to yours. Ask yourself: "Am I going to die angry? Am I going to die hurt? Am I going to die holding on to what could have been released? Am I going to pass this energy along?"

If you look back, you can probably see how this pain was transferred from your great-grandparents, into your grandparents, and into you. Now, look forward into the future. What happens if that pain stays within you? That's right, it will get passed on.

You see, here's what else you get to do: You get to be *the one.*

The one who ends the cycle for your children, grandchildren, and the rest of your line. The one who does the deep and courageous work, who ends it all. And at the same time, the one who *begins* it.

You see, the same way pain can change a generation of lives and alter destinies is the same way that love can do the same. And you get to choose. You can choose to allow the pain to remain within, or you can choose to release it. And you can choose to allow love to take its place.

Now, choosing doesn't mean you have to take action, it just means you choose to open yourself to letting go, to allowing the process to take place.

What if this is it? What if the secret of life—of healing, moving forward, and returning to our heart—is simply allowing ourselves to let go of *every* bit of resistance, fear, and unforgiveness that we're holding within? What if it's about letting go of everything—every story, limiting belief, and low-frequency energy that was ever imprinted onto us or born out of the pain trapped inside our parents? What if it's always been about living, not from the fear of the mind, but from the love of the heart?

AWAKEN YOU
The Letter

I recently had a channeling session with Source where I was told to write a specific letter to my mother and father. I was told writing this letter would change everything for me, and it did. Now, I'd like to give you the opportunity to write the same letter to your mother and father:

Write a short letter to your mother and one to your father. Be sure to write a separate letter to each. In it, say anything that you would not or could not say to them. It's your opportunity to fully get it all out. Thank them for giving you the most beautiful gift anyone can ever give, the gift of life.

Thank them each for the gifts they've given you to make you into the magnificent being you are. Because that's what you are, magnificent!

If either of them is no longer here, tell them you were not ready for them to go as early as they did.

Tell them you love them and apologize for not always accepting them exactly as they individually were or are. Write that you release all conscious or unconscious resentments or negative energy toward them. Read it out loud, and then sit in front of a fire and burn it.

PART III

TRANSFORM

CHAPTER 8

THE THREE ENERGIES OF HUMAN MASTERY

I called my first in-person events Relentless, and back then, they were mainly for real estate professionals. For years, agents and brokers called me asking if I'd coach them on how to increase sales and become better entrepreneurs. What they really were searching for—many without realizing it—was help transforming their lives. So after I sold my real estate company, I figured the next obvious step was to get into coaching.

I didn't want it to be only about real estate fundamentals, though. I wanted to share some of the healing and energy work I was learning about too, so the coaching company I created did both. I talked about real estate *and* the actions people needed to take to improve their business. More importantly, I spoke about energy and the inner work needed to truly transform their lives.

Yet something about the event didn't feel quite right.

Consider the word *relentless*. As you say it, *feel* the energy of that word. When you think back to the chapters on healing, and about what you've learned, what is the energy behind *relentless*? It's forcing, going after, constant motion, never ending.

It's all masculine. Masculine, as we've talked about, isn't wrong, but when it's unbalanced and there's no feminine, then we're stuck in doing, grinding, and hustling. That is exactly the energy most people in real estate are in.

I didn't understand this much about energy back when I first started Relentless. I definitely didn't understand that even the name of an event can carry energy. Yet the more I awakened, and the deeper I went within, the more I came to this life-changing realization:

There's nothing to be relentless about! And there is nothing to chase, because a real abundant life isn't lived from the outside in; it's lived from the inside out.

So there it was in December 2021, and I was hosting Relentless IV in Los Angeles. I had almost 1,200 people packed into the Anaheim Hilton Ballroom, and it was on fire. Everything flowed beautifully, and there was an undeniable energy you could feel in the room.

As I looked out at the crowd, I felt like the king. I had conquered the game of real estate. I mastered how to play it, and now I was teaching others to do the same. My coaching company was thriving. I had a waiting list for clients that would keep me busy for years.

Yet I couldn't shake the feeling that I was still playing safe, that there was more I was being called to become, more I was being called to unravel, and more I was being called to offer to others.

I had one foot in and one out, and I felt confused. I was on my spiritual journey, learning so much about life, the illusion of separation, oneness, about how we create our lives, energy, and what it takes to heal. All of it felt magical to me, it felt like my purpose, my truth, yet I kept asking myself, *What does any of this have to do with real estate?*

I knew I had the ability to guide people through deep awakening and healing, yet I was stuck in a box that was labeled "real estate coach." A box I created for myself, because my identity was so connected to being "a real estate guy."

To change our lives, we have to have the courage to climb out of whatever unconscious box we're living in and whatever identity it has trapped us in.

All weekend long at Relentless, questions kept flowing into me, questions that forced me to think about what I really wanted for myself and life. *Who do I want to be? What do I want to help people see? How do I want to spend my time each day? Who do I want to be with?*

Finally, *what do I want?*

It wasn't about what I thought I *should* want. I wanted to know what my heart and soul wanted for me. I wanted to know my life's path.

WHAT DO YOU WANT?

Up until now, we've talked mainly about awakening and healing. Now it's time to step into the masculine and ignite transformation. First, you must gain clarity around what you want and what you need to let go of to make space for the new you and new life to be born.

So, with your eyes closed, ask yourself: *What will make me happy? What do I want to create or call into my life?*

For a lot of people, answering these questions is hard. Most of us don't actually want what we think we want, or what we think will make us happy. We want what the world tells us to want, or what we've been programmed to want. Since we were young, we've had ads, billboards, social media, television, and movies bombarding us with these ideas of what a "great" life should look like. As a result, we become disconnected from our inner truth, so when we ask ourselves questions like "What will make me happy?" or "What do I want?" we simply don't know.

When I ask you to consider what will make you happy and what you want, I'm asking you to answer from your heart, from your highest self.

You're here. You're alive. And you're having this beautiful experience called life. You know now that you are the creator of it all, and there are no limits to what you can create. So what kind of life would actually make you happy? What would fulfill you? What would bring you deep inner peace?

Forget about everyone else and focus on *you*, on what's coming from your heart. Have you ever allowed yourself to stop and ask yourself this question and get granular about the life you want to live?

Not based on the unconscious box you live in. Not based on the parents you were born to, the family you were born into, the color of your skin, the money in your bank account, where you currently live, any unconscious cultural restraints, or your current situation.

Forget about it all. Forget about who you "think" you are, what you "think" is expected of you, or what you "think" you should want.

If you're unhappy in your life or where it's headed, then please know that it was created from the pre-healed version of you. You called in a life to match the frequency of the old you.

Now, you're different.

This book has already caused you to go inward, something you may have never done before, and just by reading these words, by taking in the energy of these messages, things are starting to open up inside of you. And if you're not feeling this, it's okay. Just pause, and trust that all the work you've done until this point has started to energetically upgrade you, because it has.

You've begun letting go of some of what's been holding you back, and as a result, you're now making space for the abundance you seek to come to you. With every release, you raise your consciousness. You begin vibrating at a higher energetic level, which by default means you're making space for the future you want to call in.

What I'm talking about is real spirituality. It's not looking a certain way, becoming a guru, or being able to meditate for an hour. It's healing and living an abundant life based on your truth. It's returning to you—the whole you. To the center of you. When you do this, you become *free* to create the life that you want. And you begin the journey of becoming aware of whatever is holding you back, and whereas before you lived with it, now you face it, go into it, and heal it and the energy associated with it. You do this over and over again until one day, you are living the very life you are calling in today.

This is living from the inside out. Where the inner work creates the outer life.

THE THREE ENERGIES OF HUMAN MASTERY

So if most of us don't actually know what we want or what will make us happy, how do we find the truth? I've found it helpful to start this journey by looking at what I call the *Three Energies of Human Mastery*:

1. Food
2. Money
3. Sex

To experience a fulfilled and balanced life, we need to align these three areas with the deepest parts of our inner being. (Plus, almost everyone, at some point on their journey, wants to experience transformation in one or more of them.)

These three energies will challenge you, and are incredible teachers and medicine. The more you want to create and become in each of them, the more limitations they'll force you to face, and the more you get to become by facing them.

You'll have no choice but to ask yourself, "What am I going to do about my inner blocks? Will I allow them to keep me from experiencing a life of alignment, joy, and freedom? Do I want to change so badly that the word *creator* is no longer a word, but something I choose to embody?"

Every insecurity, every inadequacy, and every limitation you've been taught to believe about yourself will get drawn out as you begin working with the energy of food, money, and sex.

Simultaneously, these three energies will give you the opportunity to transcend, grow, and create the life of your dreams. They represent the fundamental forces within that you must understand, balance, and embody to achieve true mastery over your life.

FOOD

How we nourish ourselves reflects to us our connection to the feminine, our mother, and our emotional well-being, as the mother's breast is the original source of nourishment and life.

So if in our relationship with our mother, we did not find the nurturing, love, care, soothing, comfort, or kindness our hearts desired, then we could potentially search for it in other ways. When this happens, a part of us is unquenched or unsatisfied: It continues to seek nourishment, care, comfort, and love. And a lot of us unconsciously use food to help fill that desire.

Our relationship with food mirrors our relationship with ourselves and our mothers, as it's the mother who teaches us how to relate to ourselves. If we have peace and contentment within, then we will have peace and contentment with food. If we have ease within ourselves, we will have ease with food.

Our relationship with food also directly ties to our relationship with life itself.

The world tells us to scroll on social media, watch television and movies, and look at ads to understand how our body "should" look, and that our value is in its size and shape. As a result, many of us carry unrealized shame about our bodies—the very temple housing our soul. If we carry shame toward our body, we carry shame toward our life.

Some carry extra weight to create an extra layer of barrier between themselves and others. This is typically a sign of feeling unsafe, or in cases of sexual abuse, wanting to look unattractive in order to never again attract the wrong kind of attention.

If you've never understood why you carry extra weight or over- or undereat, can you open the space within to ask yourself why? Can you look within to see if there are unhealed wounds around your feminine? Your relationship to your mother? Can you become aware of how you unconsciously look for food to quench something that may be deep within and unresolved? Whatever you discover, set an intention around it and use the free breathwork in the previous chapter to begin the process of healing it.

MONEY

What if nothing was expensive? What if there was no such word? What if everything is simply a match, or not, to the frequency inside of us? What if, all along, money has just been energy?

Because that's all it actually is. Money is energy, and it can flow in and out of your life like anything else. You've been told money is about what you're doing and the effort you put into getting it. What if that's only half the truth?

What if money has always been about who you're *being,* and it flows into your life based on who you *are and what you actually believe you're worthy of receiving*? Not the masks you wear, but the actual essence you vibrate at—the real you. Money has been meeting you there all along, and will continue to do so. Heal the energy, you heal the money.

In my early years in real estate, I thought money was about what I was doing, how much hustle and effort I put in, because when I looked around, that was (and for many people still is) the system I saw everyone lived in. But I hated the stress and strain it placed on me, and so one day, I simply decided to challenge that system by playing a different game. I decided to tap into the energy of the impossible, the same energy I used at the age of 18 when I declared, "I will buy my mom a house by 21."

I decided to state the impossible again: "I will create a billion-dollar sales company while only working five hours a week or less."

Making that statement made me confront every part of me which didn't believe I was worthy of that reality. For the next three years, I focused on upgrading my essence, my beliefs, and my energy until the statement became a vibrational match for myself. Every time fear came up about expanding my business, hiring new people, and the massive responsibility of it, I faced it. I faced the parts of me that were afraid, the same way I'm asking you to do now. Within four years, I created the impossible—a billion-dollar sales company.

Money has never been about what you do. It has always been about who you *are*. You want to upgrade your money? Upgrade the energy within you. When you're in that space, aligned with your highest self, or at minimum on the journey of alignment, money has no choice but to show up. Why? Because it is a match for the frequency of love, expansion, and truth. That's the currency of the Universe. It's not fear. It's not lack. It's not scarcity.

The energy of the Universe is resonance. It's *abundance and love.*

Have you ever wondered why you feel a ceiling, a block, or a gap between what you want and what's in your bank account? Look deeper. Not in the world. Not in the economy. Not toward someone to blame for your circumstance. Look within. What are you still saying to yourself, silently, that keeps you small? What stories are still playing on repeat, like "I'm not worthy." "I'll never get ahead." "I always mess it up." "It's selfish to want more." "There's never enough."

These thoughts don't just shape your mood. They literally recalibrate and reinforce a frequency living within you. And since you are the creator of your life, and everything is *one*, the Universe has no choice but to simply send you whatever vibrates at the same frequency of the words that live within you.

So what if you allowed yourself to start telling yourself a new story? Could you find the space for that? The same way we worked on letting go of the pain of your mom and dad, can you let go of the pain of these harmful words and create a new story? One rooted in your authentic truth, not the truth someone else or some system gave to you? The truth your heart and soul knows and is now ready to accept and realign with?

To ignite this shift, say the following out loud in a clear, strong, and powerful voice:

> *"I am enough. I am abundant. Life supports me. Money is energy. I am energy, therefore (drumroll and holy shit moment!)* I am money!"

Again, when you're ready, use the free breathwork in the previous chapter to go into ceremony and heal whatever resistance is coming up when you say these statements.

When you live from this frequency, when you love yourself fully, when you walk with life instead of against it, money is no longer a "goal." It's simply a byproduct of alignment. It becomes a sacred mirror of how deeply you are choosing to show up as the real you.

So stop chasing money. Start choosing you.

And the floodgates of abundance will open up and follow.

SEX

When it comes to the act of sex, humans have serious hangups as a result of how society and religion have conditioned us. And yet sex is the thing that God gave us to create life. It's the portal of life, the embodiment of pleasure, and the expression of our creative essence.

Let's pause here for a second to talk about religion and sex. So much of the guilt and shame we carry around sex comes from teachings that were passed down through religion, or through families impacted by those teachings. Shame around sex is one of the main energies we help people clear at AWAKEN.

Take the story of Adam and Eve that we looked at in Chapter 5: At its heart, it's a story of separation. Separation between the masculine and the feminine, between humans and nature, and between us and our kundalini energy symbolized by the serpent. That serpent is actually symbolic of our ability to awaken our life force, chakras, and to know ourselves through pleasure.

Once you label the source of life as sinful, then it becomes very easy to manipulate and control human life. Because through the mind, you can eventually control people's bodies, desires, instincts, and, eventually, their souls. That is why you are told lots of things about sex, like what you can and can't do. It's why there is so much shame around masturbation, which is connecting with yourself in pleasure. It's why you're told Jesus was born to a virgin, and why you're told that sex before marriage is a sin.

Here's a truth you might not be ready for, yet I love you enough to stand in truth and tell it to you: There is no such thing as sin. There's only energy, and it's either aligned with life or it isn't. Animals don't sin. Neither do trees. Nor does the Earth, and yet they're all sacred, as are you. I didn't say people don't do bad things; why they do them is for another book. The truth is, the only reason you feel like a sinner is because your mind was trained to believe you are. That belief carried an unconscious cycle of hiding, shame, and secrecy around the most natural thing in the world: your sexual energy.

This gets really deep, because if you believe that sex is sin, or have any shame at all around it, then you grow up interacting with sex from a very hidden and dark place. This opens you to feeling shame around your body versus freedom and love for it. Most of us grew up masturbating and having sex in secret, afraid to speak about our experiences, because we'd be judged.

Yet, sex is the very thing that your body and soul feels is natural. It's literally what created you. If you feel shame around the act that created you, then you will unconsciously feel shame around *creation and life itself.*

Sex is the very thing that your body and soul feels is natural. It's what created you. Yet, if you feel shame around the act that created you, then you will feel shame around creation and life itself.

And it goes even deeper. When someone experiences sexual trauma, whether through abuse, manipulation, or even emotional suppression, the lower chakras begin to close. This is where our life force lives; our grounding and our safety are all connected to our lower energy centers, as those are the closest to the connection to the Earth. When they're blocked, they may feel stuck in survival mode, disconnected from their body, from joy, and from their own sense of power.

Hopefully, you can now see that healing your relationship with sex is not just about having better sex (though that's an incredible byproduct). It's about reclaiming your creativity, safety, joy, and connection to life.

I invite you to observe what's coming up for you right now. Don't judge, resist, or avoid it. Just breathe and notice it. Let it rise to the surface. Remember it's all just energy, which you're free to keep, release, or change.

When I started to understand this, it was a lot for me to take in. I was the guy often harping on everyone else and saying that sex, outside of marriage, was a sin. I felt so righteous telling people they were wrong, when secretly, inside of myself, I was stuck in deep addiction to pornography. All because shame and guilt was trapped within me, especially around sex and my body. So what do you do when you're living in those lower energies? You *do* things to make you feel more guilty and shameful.

If you're reading this and realizing "That's me. I've been carrying this shame. I've been disconnected," then please know, it's okay. Just pause for a moment and take a breath. Place a hand on your heart or your lower belly, or maybe even your heart and sex organs, and speak gently to yourself:

"I am Safe. I am Pleasure. I am Joy. I am Love. I am Free."

When you're ready, write a letter to your body, or to your younger self, around the time when you first remember feeling ashamed of your sexual energy. Let that part of you speak. Let it say everything it never had permission to say. And when you're done, don't analyze it, just breathe.

Through this one act, you will help to release stored energy while taking back your power.

A Portal to Divine Connection

What no one teaches us is that sex is far more than just a physical act—it's a portal to creation and divine connection, and it's a mirror to how we are in life.

So if you're restricted in the act of sex, could you also be restricted in life?

If you're afraid during the act of sex, could you also be afraid in life?

If you're abusive in the act of sex, then could you also be abusive in life?

If you're rigid in sex, could you also be rigid in life?

If you're constantly overthinking during sex, then could you also constantly be overthinking in life?

If you're stressed and worried while having sex, could you also be stressed and worried in life?

Sex is miraculous. It's beautiful. It creates life. It created *you*. When you can finally allow yourself to be liberated, to own it, feel it, to give and receive openly, to express and feel deliciously, you will be free.

Relationships and Love

While I used sex in the examples above, I could easily replace that with the word *relationship* or *love*. Because how we are in our relationships is how we are in relation to life and to ourselves.

Sex is the deepest point of connection we have with another human being. If we allow it, it can be the moment when all our deepest and most protective walls fall, our masks drop, and our soul gets the wonderful opportunity to truly meet another soul, in love, truth, vulnerability, and essence.

But again, only if we allow it.

There's that word again, *allow*, which is feminine. Because just like life, we can rush through sex, using it to avoid what we really feel. Or we can let it become a doorway and portal back to trust, oneness, and love. When two people enter into sexual union with presence, intention, and love instead of performance, pressure, and programming, then *sex becomes sacred.*

In that space, the energy exchanged is not just physical, it's spiritual, healing, and magnetic. In fact, sex can become just as, if not more, healing than any of the medicines I mentioned in the last chapter, because it brings to the surface what's still unhealed, and gives it a place to be seen, felt, held, and released.

This is why sex can be the *most healing thing in your relationship.* If you can be safe here, you can be safe anywhere. If you can feel love in it, you can allow love in life. If you can open here, you can open yourself to all that life truly has to offer you.

ENERGIES INTERTWINING

The Three Energies of Human Mastery intertwine, because everything is connected. You see, food ties to our self-worth; so does money and our relationships.

With food, for example, let's talk about buying organic versus non-organic, which is based on our self-worth. I know what your mind is thinking. It's probably going, "No, it's based on what I can afford."

Question for you: What if you valued yourself so much that you were willing to starve unless you had the best quality food available on the planet? Wouldn't that naturally motivate, inspire, and uplift you so you find a way to make the money you need to match the commitment of only putting the best in your body? So what if, all along, one of the secrets to making more money is in the quality of the food you eat? Which is directly connected to how much you love and value yourself?

Now here comes relationships. What if one of the secrets to attracting the partner of your dreams is in the food that you decide to eat as well? Because how could you ever find a partner who will honor you if you don't honor yourself with the food that you put into your body? And if you allow second best into your life with food, then you'll receive second best in all areas of your life, including your relationships.

So the food you eat is simply an external reflection for the energy that you're living with within you, and for the love that you have for yourself.

This works not only with the quality of food but the quantity too. When you overeat, it might be because there's something inside of you asking for more of what you never received as a baby or child—more peace, soothing, love. Maybe all along it's the feminine within you that's craving, not that you "have a sweet tooth."

If you have an issue with food, it's not that you're bad, undisciplined, or lazy. No, it's not any of that. It's that a part of your heart was broken at some point in your life. Maybe no one has told you that. That's perfectly okay. Your future self called in this book to finally make you aware so the healing process can begin.

Set an intention around what came up in this section to heal and go into ceremony with the breathwork to begin releasing it.

SO, WHAT DO YOU REALLY WANT?

The reason you're struggling in relation to your health and food, money, and relationships and sex is because you don't believe you have the power to decide that you—and your life—can be different.

It can.

The awakening and healing you do will start the process. Transformation begins by getting crystal clear.

So, I'll ask again, what do you *really* want, when it comes to the Three Energies of Human Mastery?

The world tells you that you have to go do something to get what you want. What I'm telling you is that the real magic happens before you do anything at all. It's in crystal clarity in the decision. It's in seeing it happen in your mind's eye before it happens. That's how you create. The same way you've been seeing what could go wrong, from this day forward you see all that could and as a result will go right.

The magic is in telling the Universe what you want, envisioning and feeling it as if it were already here, and then just surrendering, letting go, and watching it all unfold.

To help ignite this transformation, I'm going to walk through each of the Three Energies of Human Mastery. I invite you to journal what you want. No holding back. No restrictions.

Food

Your number one priority in life, above money, above relationships, above everything is your physical wellness, vitality, and longevity. Without it, you won't be here to enjoy anything else.

One of the main issues in society today is that we place money or relationships first. We put our business, work, relationship or partner, even our kids, before ourselves. As a result, we accept unnecessary stress, which can often lead to unnecessary illness. Think about the people you work with and for, your partner, or your past partner. Has your physical well-being ever been impacted by them? How many bosses have you worked for who were rude to you, clients you've had who caused you stress, partners you've been with who were regularly emotionally disruptive?

Here's the deeper question: What price did your body have to pay as a result?

When we don't honor our body, we send a message to the Universe to not honor us or our heart's desire. Because we show that we're willing to accept the crumbs when the entire buffet is available.

Raise your right hand and place your left over your heart and repeat after me:

> *"From this day forward, I come first. From this day forward, nothing comes before my peace and well-being. From this day forward, my well-being is my top priority."*

Now, let's get clear. Ask and answer the following questions:

- How do I want to feel in my body?
- What do I want my health to feel like?
- What do I want to change about my relationship with my body and/or food?

When you put yourself and well-being first, you open yourself to real alignment in the next two energies.

Money

When it came to money and my finances, I wanted to live life on my terms, doing what I wanted with who I wanted, where I wanted, when I wanted, and how I wanted. I wanted to get paid to exist, to never feel like I'm working a day in my life. When you're living from your highest self, you don't work. You just are. The Universe pays you to exist.

And I'm reminding you of this because I'm saying this as someone whom society considers "a minority." I grew up in the ghetto, living on food stamps and public assistance. Yet I did what I'm teaching you to do in this book. I stopped hoping, stopped wondering how life would change, and I *decided* it would.

You have the freedom and ability to do the same.

So decide and declare right now: *"What will my financial life look like in the next 10 years?"*

If you need some help and inspiration in allowing your heart to show you what you want for alignment with money, then consider the *Five Levels of Financial Freedom.*

Level 1: Freedom from $5 Worries

This is the energy of never having to worry about affording something that costs as little as $5. For a lot of us, that hasn't always been the story. I remember going to the grocery store, feeling constantly worried that the cashier would tell me I didn't have enough money. After the housing market crashed, and I lost everything, this was the feeling I lived with for almost two years. Not having the ability to afford groceries for my family was life changing. It showed me what I never wanted to experience again when it came to money.

Level 2: Freedom to Ask Six-Figure Questions

When you're in alignment with money (which, remember, is simply energy), you are never limited. It affords you the freedom to ask these six-figure questions about how you want to live your life and how you want it to look. What kind of home do you want to live in? Where do you want to live? How do you want to travel?

Level 3: Freedom from Location

This is the ability to live and work anywhere in the world, to be free to come and go as you please. This doesn't mean you have to live and work around the world. It's the freedom to decide, because no job controls you. No boss dictates where you have to live. You get to decide.

Level 4: Freedom from Time Limits

Do you dream of having a flexible work schedule? Setting your own hours? Or maybe clocking in every Monday through Friday from 9 A.M. to 5 P.M. Guess what? There's no right or wrong answer, but wouldn't it be nice if you were the one to decide?

This is the freedom to do what you want, when you want. Now, I'm not saying this removes any responsibilities or obligations you have to other people and commitments you've made at work or at home. It means you have the freedom to decide—to choose—rather than constantly being forced into a situation that you don't want to be in any longer, if ever.

Level 5: Freedom from Expectations

This is the ability to completely craft your own abundant and aligned life based on no one else but your authentic self.

Get clear, and let your truth come out onto the page. This is the moment you create a new financial future.

Sex and Relationships

The movie *The Notebook*, starring Ryan Gosling and Rachel McAdams, changed everything for me, because it showed me what was possible when it came to love. I grew up never really seeing any examples of happy, passionate love in the couples I knew. Once I saw that film, I created an affirmation that I believe helped me attract my beautiful wife, Jen.

That affirmation? "*The Notebook* or bust."

That movie showed me exactly what I wanted: a dream partner. I wanted to get past the butterfly stage that I would always feel in the first 30 days, which I mistook for love.

Yet how do you know when you've found *the one forever* or just the *one for right now*? What does it mean to want a partner or a healthy relationship? Jen and I talk about this a lot, especially on our podcast, *Finding the One*.

Understanding the difference is something that I call *PPV*—short for Presence, Personality, and Values.

Presence

The most important things to look for in a partner are the traits found within. That doesn't mean you have to bypass what you're physically attracted to. But it does mean going deeper than the outside. So write in detail the presence your dream partner gives off. What's their style? What's the energy they exude when they walk in a room? What's their look? Get as crystal clear as possible.

Personality

All your exes have shown you what you *don't* want. There's nothing worse than being with someone whose natural way of being causes unnecessary conflict or unhappiness. Here's the good news: That ex came into your life to show you what you don't want and to make it evidently clear what you do want.

So what do you want their personality and energy to feel like? Are they confident? Quiet? Outspoken? Are they fun to be with and around? What traits in your partner would cause you to feel at peace and in joy in their presence?

The clearer you are, the more likely you'll be to call them in.

Values

What do you want your partner to value in life? Will they be on the healing journey with you, valuing their spirituality and connecting with their highest self too? Will family be important to them? Will their career? Will being financially free? How will they want to, or how do they, raise kids? (That's presuming you want or have children.)

Be clear about the values you want in your partner.

* * *

If you're with someone, then return to your lists and give them a 0 to 10 rating in each category, meaning how well do they match up with what you said you wanted?

Now, only commit yourself to a serious relationship with someone who is a nine or above in each category. If they're not, I'm not suggesting you race out to break up or divorce them, although that might be the path for you, eventually. This is about getting clear on your dream partner, and if you're not with that person, going deep within you to ask *why*.

As I said, it might be that the relationship doesn't work and it's time to move on. This happened with my first wife.

It also might mean that the relationship is important, this is your dream partner, but you have to become the person who you've described in the PPV. When you change your vibration, then either your partner will also energetically change to meet you, the relationship will run its course, or you'll call in the partner who does.

LETTING GO

If you take only one message away from this book, I hope it's the knowledge that you truly are the creator of your life. Writing what your heart and soul wants means it's already yours. Now, it's about going on the journey of *becoming* the person who vibrates at the level of what you want. This journey is about unraveling whatever it is that's stopping or blocking you from creating what you want.

You see, the clearer you become on what you want and what will make your heart happy, the clearer you also become on what's stopping or blocking you from that life.

Which brings us again to healing. The more you heal, the more you make space for God's light to shine within. The less energy we put on things and people that no longer serve us, the more energy and space we have to take action when our heart and soul direct us and to attract and receive everything that we want in life.

That's why healing is the most important thing that you can do in your life, because it's a process of letting go of everything you've unconsciously put your God-given power and energy into that's been blocking you from everything you want.

Now that you know what you want, it's time to ask yourself: *"What do I need to let go of and heal so that I can become whole and complete?"*

I've had to let go of a lot on this journey of transformation. For one, I had to let go of the Relentless events and my niche business coaching real estate professionals in order to make space for everything I'm experiencing in my life now. Maybe you need to let go of something big too, like a relationship or a job.

Whatever is pinging your heart right now as you read these words, it's because deep inside of you, a part of you has always known that there is something that hasn't, or no longer, serves you.

And it's okay if you start small, like letting go of one particular food that you will no longer put into your body, or simply bringing awareness to what it is that you will release. I actually teach people to start with something easy to let go of and build up to the big stuff, because it gives your mind a chance to get more comfortable with you stepping outside of the illusion of safety and into the unknown, which is where the real abundance lives.

- **Health and Food:** What do you need to let go of when it comes to your health and the food you eat?
- **Money:** What do you need to let go of with money?
- **Sex and Relationships:** What do you need to let go of in sex and/or in relationships?

FORGET HOW

For well over a year, I found myself constantly asking, "What do I want?" and "What will make me happy?" I thought a lot about what I wanted to feel in my body, the foods I would fuel myself with, and what health meant for me. I thought about what I wanted to earn for money and how I wanted my financial life to look and feel. I thought about finding a partner and what I wanted my relationship to be like. Finally, I thought about everything that I needed to let go of, from thoughts and beliefs to habits, behaviors, my lifestyle, possessions, relationships, even my business and work. Nothing escaped examination.

All of these questions and answers rattled within me for more than a year before I did anything. It took that long, because I was scared to let go of everything I knew and who I was. One day at an event just like Relentless, I decided it was time to give up and surrender to what I was being called to.

So I stood onstage to thank everyone for coming, and I told them about my future.

"From this day forward, we will no longer be called a real estate coaching company, so this will be the last ever event in this space. I don't know what we're going to be as a company. I just know there's more to life for me than talking about real estate."

It was a blur after that. I know I must have thanked everyone and wished them well, yet all I could think about as I walked offstage was how free it felt to finally speak my truth. I no longer wanted to focus solely on real estate, and I didn't want to only help real estate professionals grow their businesses. I knew I wanted more for my life and that I felt pulled to talk about awakening on a spiritual and soul level. So I was determined to go forward in that direction.

It didn't matter what the decision would cost me or how much business I'd lose. At that moment, my entire livelihood depended on my real estate coaching business, and there I was torpedoing my only income without knowing what exactly was next, or how I'd replace my work.

The only thing I knew was that to live in freedom and inner peace, I had to be willing to let go of the real estate part of me and my life. I had to let my identity as "the real estate guy" die for the new me to be born.

And I had to release the need to know *how* everything would work out.

"How?" is the greatest prison of your life.

You have a vision about what you want to accomplish or change in your life—maybe it's a more intimate relationship, better sex, to make more money, or to lose weight and feel better in your body—and I guarantee, the first question your mind will ask is, "How?"

And suddenly you stop, and it—the awakening, healing, and transformation—all ends right there.

The trick to life is understanding that you are so powerful that your relationship to the word *how* is the doorway to creating the ultimate vision for your life.

You just have to transmute the relationship. Where once the question "How?" stopped you, you now get the opportunity to tap into a place where you can say, "How no longer matters. What matters more to me is 'Why?'" Because if your why is important enough, you'll figure out the how—and you won't do it alone. You'll receive guidance and inspiration from your highest self, intuition, angels, spirit guides, ancestors, God, you name it.

When I told the audience I was done, I didn't know "how" I was going to transition the company. I didn't have a business plan or vision for how this new life as a spiritual guide would grow. I just knew I had to expand beyond the real estate sector. I knew I was being called to something more, and I could sense that by taking a step in that direction, everything else in my life, from my health and body to my finances and relationships, would also move too. It did, in time.

What keeps us stuck in life is that we expect everything to align *perfectly* before we make a decision. As if the Universe is supposed to show us a sign that everything is going to be okay or give us exactly what we need before we need it.

Actually, it's the opposite.

You *decide* and *then* the Universe conspires to bring you everything you need based on the decision. Quite literally, the how doesn't matter. The decision is the only thing that does, and it's the one thing that immediately shifts timelines in your favor.

You can make as much money as you want working as little as you want.

You can attract your dream relationship.

You can have your dream body and health.

Will it take having to change some things about yourself? Absolutely. That's the juice in the journey of life!

You've lived your entire life needing to know "How?" Yet all of life will open for you if you can let go of the need to know the answers to that question and every step that you'll take to create the life you want, the one that will make you truly happy. It will happen, step by step. And it only gets revealed along the way at exactly the right time.

Remember how in Chapter 1 I told you my former pastor said if I divorced my wife, then I would lose all of God's blessings? And remember how I said earlier in this chapter that I got onstage at Relentless and said, "From this day forward, we will no longer be a real estate coaching company"?

Would you agree, if it wasn't for those two decisions, I never would have become the man who would do this spiritual and coaching work or even write this book?

I have never seen every step along my journey. I've only ever seen the next step or the next decision.

What if you don't need to know all the steps or decisions either? Maybe, just maybe, the Universe, Source, God, Life is waiting for you to decide to transform, to decide that from this day forward, you will leave the energy of fear to create whatever it is your heart and soul want.

What if it's that simple? What if all you have to do is decide? What if that decision is the thing you have to "do" that shifts the energy within that changes the course of your life, forever?

What if that decision is the thing you have to "do" that shifts the energy within that changes the course of your life, forever?

Every time I've faced a moment, or a decision, to leave fear and go into love, to listen to my heart and soul, I've said, "I'm all in." And there's something about making that decision that ignites the fire inside. It kindles a trust in you, a trust in life, and a trust in God to call in and create the thing that your heart wants.

So what is it you want?

Be clear.

Be decisive.

Be true to you.

AWAKEN YOU
Transformation Prayer

Close your eyes, and take three deep breaths in, focusing only on the inhales and exhales. Then say the following prayer out loud once, and then silently with your eyes closed, and sit in stillness for at least two minutes.

"God, I'm ready to transform my life. I'm ready to face whatever I need to face. I'm ready to become my highest version of myself. I open myself to your guidance. Show me the path. Bring to me all of the lessons, people, circumstances, and help I'll need on this journey. Make the pathway clear, and I will follow it. Today I decide. Today I begin a new life. Today, I am the very abundance I call into existence."

CHAPTER 9

A LIFE UNLIMITED

My roots are Dominican and Ecuadorian, yet I was born in New York City and lived there until I turned 13, so that may have made me (unofficially) Puerto Rican. Then I moved to California, so that may have made me (unofficially) Mexican, plus we lived in the hood, so that may have made me (unofficially) Black.

Because of all these influences, when I played music, I played *everything,* but people didn't understand.

"You have a confused playlist," was common for me to hear whenever I played my music around others.

"I like it all," I'd say, not understanding the "problem."

Even at a young age, we're taught that people with certain skin color, ancestry, cultures, and ethnicities listened to specific music. And, yes, there are ancestral lineages, traditions, and reasons why types of music came into being. Yet it's also just another way separation keeps us divided.

I remember as a kid thinking that one day, I wanted to have a big party where I could play all of my favorite songs and everyone would dance. I never forgot this. It turns out that my live events are that party.

At 9 A.M. on the third day of AWAKEN, we have an hour-long dance party where I play everything from pop to country, rap, and, of course, salsa and Mariachi. Not only are we moving the energy in our bodies through dance, we're having fun, letting loose, and feeling free to be ourselves. Usually it takes some warming up for this to happen. Initially people seem awkward and self-conscious. There's a lot of gentle swaying and head nodding.

But not from me. I go for it. I sing, dance, and probably look like a maniac, yet by day three, most people are used to me. They've seen me jumping off the stage, walking among the crowd, sitting cross-legged on the floor, swearing, laughing, and singing all while speaking in Spanish and English.

I'm just being me without limits or worries about how people will see me. This combined with the music gives people permission to do the same—to be free, to sing, dance, smile, laugh, and just *be* themselves without restrictions. Eventually, during our dance party, I see the awkwardness drop, the insecurity and self-consciousness vanish, and people get lost in the music, rhythm, and the feeling of being alive—of being themselves. In that moment, the morning of day three at AWAKEN, music causes all barriers to cease existing and in an instant we all become *one*.

Yet, there was one event where no matter what song I played, one woman couldn't let loose, dance, or even smile. Every song I chose, my eyes would quickly scan her, waiting for some sign that I'd hit her heart. Nothing I played seemed to strike, and as the hour crept closer to ending, I began to worry that she wouldn't have her moment.

Until I turned on a Whitney Houston song and there she was! Beaming, dancing, laughing.

In that moment she let go, and by doing so, she graced the entire room with the most dazzling, brilliant smile. I felt her energy suddenly go up five notches, and she was shining.

WHAT HOLDS US BACK

What stopped that woman from singing, dancing, and having a good time? It's possible she hated my playlist, yet in my experience, the issue was deeper. Likely, it was the negative thoughts and limiting beliefs she had unconsciously allowed to live inside of her.

We're born without limiting beliefs and negative stories, yet we create them to unconsciously keep us safe by avoiding the pain we once felt as children. We also absorb them through whatever our parents, caretakers, and society feed to us.

What we absorb, we end up believing.

What we end up believing, we end up becoming.

And what we end up becoming reinforces what we see and experience in the world.

You may recall the projector we mentioned earlier in the book. To quickly recap, it's based on the idea that we are constantly projecting into the world what we feel deeply within ourselves. So we literally see and experience life based on what we feel. For example, if you feel fear and limitation, then you will project that onto the world, calling in the people, places, jobs, and even home and location to live in to energetically match. As a result, you will continue to call into your life the very things that will keep you in the frequency of separation and fear.

I'm not talking only in a spiritual sense. Science has found that within our brain is something called the reticular activating system (RAS), which is responsible for keeping us awake and conscious, and for our sensory processing, attention, and focus. Known as a gatekeeper between our conscious mind and unconscious brain, our RAS will sift through everything that happens to us during the day to shine a light on what we consciously notice. For example, if you believe the world is a loving, supportive place, then you will notice and experience signs of love like couples holding hands, children playing, someone holding a door open for you, a stranger smiling, things that make you feel safe in your environment, and people who mirror back love, support, and peace.

The reverse is true too. If you believe the world is frightening, then that's what you will find. Maybe you'll hear angry voices, experience aggressive drivers, and notice the people who are rude or mean. You'll recall past dangers and look for signs of it repeating all around you.

For most of us, we absorbed wounded energy, negative thoughts, and limiting beliefs when growing up. The mind is so powerful that it will do anything and everything to protect us—that's the natural function of the masculine. When we're in wounded energy, the mind overcompensates in its mission to keep us safe. But it's doing so from fear instead of love.

This is what keeps you small. If your mind believes the world is dangerous, then you see signs of danger everywhere, now you're on high alert, so you won't take risks. Risk means danger, in your mind. So you close off and shut down to what's possible in your life.

Any opportunity to get out of the box you're living in, you won't take. You won't speak up for yourself when someone challenges you or tries to control you. You won't start the business you've dreamed about for years. You won't talk to the cute woman or man you spotted in the coffee shop. You won't be vulnerable and tell your partner how you really feel, put in for the promotion, or go after any dream of your heart. In fact, your mind may not even allow you to dream, because to your wounded mind, all of this is dangerous. It could lead to being let down and hurt.

Limiting beliefs put a wall between you and all of the possibilities for your destiny. They literally limit your potential to experience the fullness and richness of life.

Look deeper, and you'll actually see something very interesting. Fear and love are the same. It's just that fear is the distorted version of love. The fear stopping you from being free is doing so to protect you. Isn't that loving in nature? What if it's time to stop judging the parts of yourself that have simply been doing their best to keep you safe all of these years? What if it's time to actually thank them?

When you start thanking the parts of yourself that created the limiting beliefs, then you begin freeing yourself. You give yourself permission to let go of the limiting belief, to climb out of whatever box you unconsciously found yourself in.

In this moment, you begin to realize: *You have boundless possibilities for how your life will take shape.*

The journey from limited to limitless, from impossible to possible begins when you start climbing out of the box, because that's when life—and God—opens to you.

All of us have blocks in our heart and soul, deep ones, preventing us from living in our highest selves. Those blocks are the limiting beliefs keeping us caged, disconnected, separated, and living in fear. What greater focus can we have in our lives than dedicating ourselves to the removal of those internal blockages, going deep within ourselves? That's what the dancing at the AWAKEN events is really all about.

I know how many people don't want to dance—mostly everyone. I'm well aware of how uncomfortable, awkward, and self-conscious it makes people feel. That's exactly why we do it! Because I also know most of us loved dancing and singing as children. We didn't need a reason to do either, we just did it. We moved, made noise, and freely expressed whatever we were feeling.

Yet what we loved, and how we loved to be in the world, was lost through the years, as we were told not to be "too loud," "too silly," or "too much." From this, our mind built a story to keep us safe that said, "Dancing is dangerous. You'll be laughed at. You'll be judged. You won't be accepted."

And that's the story we carry with us, which becomes the box we're trapped in. Yet it's not only about dancing and singing. It's everything. It's why we don't post a video on social media, speak our truth, apply for a job, start a business, say no to someone, or ask for what we need. It's not because we're lazy or unmotivated. It's because we're still operating from an old story, the one the mind wrote that says, "Don't do it. Don't be seen. This is dangerous. You'll be laughed at. You'll be judged. You won't be accepted. You might get hurt."

Does this sound familiar? Deep down, this is the fear of being seen fully and living fully. And it's not just your fear. It's inherited. Generational. Cultural. Coded into your nervous system.

But you? You're the one who chose to read this chapter, which means you're the one who gets to rewrite the code. The moment you remember this and let yourself *be* again, not for anyone else, not for their applause or approval or any of that, but *for you*, you crack something open, and in the process, you return to your heart.

WHAT ARE YOU WILLING TO ACCEPT?

What are you willing to accept?

What kinds of foods do you nourish your body with? Why do you select those foods?

What kinds of friends do you spend time with?

What type of work do you give yourself to?

How do you allow people to treat you? How do your kids talk to you or treat you? What about your partner? Parents? Siblings? Friends? How about your clients, boss, or co-workers?

When you go to an event, a sports game, concert, or even a seminar, where do you sit? Are you in the first rows, or do you choose the last four of five? If you're a back-row seater—which is what most people are—what within you causes you to believe you should be in the back when the front is available?

Stop and answer all of these questions, because your life will never change until you become aware of all you've unconsciously been accepting.

What you're willing to accept is what the Universe will always give you. What *you* will give you.

What you're willing to accept is what the Universe will give.

The minute you stop accepting nosebleeds when the front row is available is the minute your life starts to change. The minute you stop allowing someone to speak to you unkindly, disrespectfully, or rudely is the minute your life starts to change. The minute you stop allowing toxic people, foods, and work into your life is the minute your life starts to change.

Is healing and releasing the trapped energy still important? Absolutely. You still need to do the awakening and healing work. What I'm describing is more like a fork-in-the-road moment, when you get to decide that from this day forward you will no longer put yourself last. You will no longer allow yourself to be treated in a way that feels wrong.

You will no longer allow the lower energies to be present.

That's what you're saying. You're putting yourself first, and valuing yourself enough to give yourself the best, because *you are the best.* You're allowing your life and yourself to become unlimited, which is what you've always been. You've simply forgotten it beneath the limiting stories and beliefs you've carried for so long.

You've been thinking your whole life that you've been limited because of the money, your upbringing, race, religion, relationship or lack of one, the extra body weight, the prescription pills, or the chronic pain or disease. But these are just surface stories. The real limitation is *energetic agreement*—you're allowing these stories to be energetically true. You're allowing the limiting energy to remain inside.

The moment you withdraw that agreement, and you stop accepting what you've been accepting, the illusion begins dissolving.

And the minute you decide to accept more from life, the Universe blesses you with more. The greatest decision of your life is to stop limiting yourself. To stop believing all the reasons why something is impossible and start declaring why it is.

In a loud and clear voice, proclaim the following:

> *"From this day forward, I will no longer accept less. I allow more, I am more."*

This has nothing to do with race, economic class, or religion. It's an energetic decision that you're done with the self-imposed limitations that cause you to settle and accept less than you're worth. And when you step into this energy, that is what the projector of your life will begin to play back to you. An entirely new story. That is what your reticular activating system will pick up and notice more of. And this is how you start triggering synchronicity and flow in your life.

WHAT ARE YOUR LIMITING BELIEFS?

The most powerful thing you can "do" is to see the limiting beliefs you're carrying around the Three Energies of Human Mastery. Once you become aware of them, you become separate from them. Once you're separate from them, you can choose to say, "No more. I am no longer willing to accept this in my life."

Grab a pen and clean sheet of paper or notebook. You're going to write your limiting beliefs. It's not enough to think or visualize them. You need to write them down. It's one of the ways human beings create, release, and transform. When we're sitting in a ceremony with ayahuasca, the medicine makes us throw up. Which is what most people fear, yet it's actually a good thing. The throwing up is a purge of all the negative energy that has been trapped inside, and that's how we release the energy, and how it leaves the body.

By writing your limiting beliefs, you begin the process of purging that energy from inside. I invite you to go deep and be honest. The more you do, the more energy you'll allow to arise, and the more you'll allow yourself to let go and transform.

What Are Your Limiting Beliefs?

1. Health and Food: What are your limiting beliefs around your health, body, and food?

For example:

- "I'll get cancer."
- "I'll die young."
- "I'll get sick."
- "I'll always be fat" or "I'll always be skinny."
- "I have bad genes."

2. Money: What are your limiting beliefs around money?

For example:

- "They're going to steal from me."
- "Money doesn't grow on trees."
- "Money is the root of all evil."
- "If I invest my money, I'm not going to have enough."
- "'The Man' is keeping me from making money."

- "It's the government's fault I don't have money."
- "I have to work hard to make money."
- "I make money, but I can't hold on to it."
- "I don't know how to invest my money."
- "I can't have a lot of money and be spiritual."
- "I'm not supposed to talk about money or what I earn."

3. Sex and Relationships: What are your limiting beliefs around sex and relationships?

For example:

- "All men are dogs."
- "All women are gold diggers."
- "I'll never find a relationship, because I'm too fat, too old, too ugly."
- "I'll never have a child. I'm too old."
- "I'm bad at relationships."
- "Sex isn't supposed to feel good."
- "People fight in relationships."
- "No one stays faithful in relationships."
- "I'm unlovable."

Flip the Tortilla

My first business ever, I was a tortilla delivery person. I would wake up at 4 A.M. to fill my truck with tortillas. When my shift ended, I would bring home a fresh package for my family to eat. I'd warm them by flipping them over fire.

That's what we're going to do with your limiting beliefs. We're going to flip them like a tortilla, because all of life is duality. Take the limiting beliefs you identified earlier and flip them. What's the unlimited belief? That's the opposite, positive version.

1. Health and Food: What is your unlimited belief about your health and/or food?

For example:

Limited Belief → Unlimited Belief

- I am going to get cancer. → I am healthy, vibrant, and radiate great health.
- I'll die young. → I am longevity, wellness, and health, and I live a long, beautiful life.
- I'll always be fat. → I am perfect, lean, and healthy.
- I will never have big muscles or be strong. → My body is my temple: strong, flexible, and powerful.
- I have bad genes. → My genes are perfect.

2. Money: What are your unlimited beliefs around money?

Examples:

Limited Belief → Unlimited Belief

- Money doesn't grow on trees. → Money grows in thin air. Money is energy, and I am energy, so money is *me*.
- Money is the root of all evil. → Money is a beautiful expression of my heart and soul. The more money I have, the better I can do in the world.
- If I invest my money, I'm not going to have enough. → I always have more than enough.
- 'The Man' is keeping me from making money. → No one keeps me from anything. I am the creator of my life, and from this day forward I create abundance.
- I have to work hard to make money. → I get paid to exist. Work is fun, and it pays me handsomely.

- I make money, but I can't hold on to it. ➔ I allow money to come into and out of my life with ease, knowing and trusting that I always have more money than I need.
- I can't have a lot of money and be spiritual. ➔ I am spiritual; therefore, I am wealthy in every aspect of my life!

3. Sex and Relationships: What are your unlimited beliefs around sex and relationships?

For example:

Limited Belief ➔ Unlimited Belief

- All men are dogs. ➔ Men are protective, kind, and loving.
- All women are gold diggers. ➔ Women are supportive, nurturing, and loving.
- I'll never find a relationship, because I'm too fat, too old, too ugly. ➔ I am the perfect partner I've looked for, therefore the one I've been looking for is me!
- I'll never have a child. I'm too old. ➔ There are many ways to have a child, and I'm never too old to adopt.
- I'm bad at relationships. ➔ I make a great partner; I am available and open to do the work.
- Sex isn't supposed to feel good. ➔ Sex is life. I am alive. Sex is a beautiful expression of my life.
- No one stays faithful in relationships. ➔ My partner stays faithful to me because I am faithful to me.

* * *

Two choices. Two pathways. Two ways of thinking, being, and as a result *living*. It's always been in front of you.

When you've lived with the limiting belief for as long as you have, it's normal to maybe feel like it's never been a choice, you're doing something wrong, or this can't be true. I promise you . . . it is.

Can you allow it to be? Can you let yourself be patient with yourself and with life as new beliefs begin unfolding? Can you give yourself the space to slowly let go of the negative and make room for the positive?

When you write all of this, a shift starts happening, and all of life begins to conspire in your favor to help bring the life that matches the new beliefs to you. If that doesn't happen right away, that's okay. This is why this path of awakening and healing is so essential. It provides us with the tools to stay in the work, to keep on the path even when it feels hard or like things aren't happening fast enough. Most of what holds us back from creating the lives our heart and soul dream about are limiting beliefs. But even deeper than the belief is the energy underneath it, the frequency that the belief rides on. And that's why belief alone is not enough to shift a life.

Life doesn't just change because we hope it to. It changes when we decide it to. And sometimes, that movement has to happen more than once, again and again until the new pattern becomes your new path. Your new way of *being*.

It's a habit, or like a well-worn path that your feet know how to walk. By writing new unlimited beliefs, you're not simply building new thoughts, you're creating new energetic pathways.

This is why so many people return to AWAKEN again and again. It's why they sit in ceremony, commit to breathwork, and join our online events or online communities like the Collective and Inner Circle. It's why they practice yoga, and why they sit with plant and mushroom medicines multiple times.

They aren't just practices, they're portals helping to unlock the old frequency and gently installing the new one, the new thoughts, the new beliefs that eventually become the new you and the new life.

AWAKEN YOU

Reprogram Your Mind

There were a lot of exercises in this chapter. If you haven't done them yet, go back and do them now. If you want to go deeper into transforming the limiting beliefs into unlimited ones, then take a result you would like to experience in life and write it as if it's already happened.

For example, if you want to earn more money, then take the most you've ever earned in a year and multiply that by three. Then write the following statement in a journal:

"I earn _______________ a year or more."

For the next six months, every day write this statement 25 times in your journal.

This isn't about achieving the goal, it's about you becoming comfortable with the number and the energy associated with it. You're becoming one with the energy of abundance, love, and unlimited possibility. As you write this every day, you're going to see how much fear, doubt, judgment, and other negative, limiting beliefs and stories appear. How resistant you are to the number itself let alone you actually earning it. The more comfortable you become with the number, the more comfortable you become with the energy that creates money.

The reason you want to write the word *more* is because you never want to limit yourself.

Remember, you can use this with any new unlimited belief in the Three Energies of Human Mastery.

CHAPTER 10

YOU ARE THE ONE

When am I going to find a partner?

What is she going to look like?

What is she going to be like?

Where am I going to meet her?

It was early in my spiritual journey. I had only sat with ayahuasca once, maybe twice, and already my life had changed a lot. I had finalized my divorce and begun coaching real estate professionals, yet I was still desperately seeking love and a relationship.

Frankly, I was fixated on it.

Until you start to become aware, you don't realize that all of these thoughts come from a wound. For me, that was my feminine wound driving me. I was looking for a woman, something outside of me to fulfill a deep emotional hole within me.

That was the space I was in when my friend Kirk called. "Brother, please help me," he said, panic-stricken early one morning. "I couldn't sleep all night. I was sweating so much that I kept having to drink water, and all I was told was that I had to talk to you."

What is he talking about? Who told him what? He wasn't making any sense, and I asked him to slow down and tell me everything.

"I have this message, and I think it's from your mother."

"Come on," I said incredulously. *My mother? Really?* I thought he had cracked and was off his rocker.

Yet, I was kind of open to what Kirk was saying, because I was having moments when I questioned reality. *Is life real?* I'd think. Sometimes it felt like I was between worlds.

Yet, I was pretty skeptical too. This psychic stuff was all new to me, and I still had a lot of religious programming buried deep within that told me it was the world of witchcraft.

So I started testing him, asking questions only my mother would have known, like nicknames for me as a kid. And after the third or fourth correct answer, I felt the truth. It was her!

"What does she want to tell me?" I quickly asked Kirk.

"She's telling me that you have to go on a trip, and she's showing me this symbol."

Kirk drew a symbol for me in the air. It looked like a gentle wave going left to right or east to west. I had no idea what it was, so we pulled out a map of the world, and I started tracing the lines on country borders. I noticed that when we flipped the symbol to run up and down or north to south, the shape perfectly matched the border from around Guatemala and Costa Rica to Colombia.

As my finger traced the outline, it felt so right that I knew I had to go to Colombia. And so I booked a trip immediately, and did it like I had never done it before—like a hippie. I grabbed one backpack, rolled up a few T-shirts, pulled on a pair of jeans, and threw in like four pairs of underwear. Then I flew to Colombia, rented a car, and planned to just do my thing, driving around the countryside. I felt like I needed this for myself—to reconnect to my roots and ancestors.

I also felt this trip was connected to a woman from Colombia whom I was fixated on. I had this idea that my next wife would have light-brown hair, and I couldn't fathom any paradigm outside of her being Hispanic. Light-brown hair and Hispanic meant she was probably going to come from Colombia or Venezuela.

I was talking with this woman from Colombia, and I was really into her, though from the beginning, her energy felt weird. She would do or say things that didn't feel right to me, yet I was so drawn to her that I looked the other way. Almost daily, I found myself thinking, *Is she the one? Yes, she is. Wait, is she, really?* I was tormenting myself with these questions, needing to know if she was the one I had waited for my entire life.

So when I returned from my backpacking trip to Colombia, I hopped on a video call with Kirk. I had to know the truth, and he obviously had some psychic ability, so I figured he'd have insight. I told Kirk about this woman, and how it wasn't really working with her, but I needed to know.

"Is she the one?" I asked him.

There was a long pause before he answered. "I think you already know, but you need to say it."

He was right. As soon as I asked him the question, I felt the answer in my body. I was just afraid of the truth. I was so attached to believing she was the one that I didn't want to say the words aloud, and yet I couldn't hold them back either.

"She's not." And as soon as I said those two words, I started violently shaking. I hurried off the call, and the next thing I knew, I was on the floor, trembling and crying.

I began calling out to God. "If she isn't the 'one,' then who is? When am I going to find her? How am I going to meet her?"

I was tired of all the questions, all the searching, and I wanted answers. Answers I never got during my time in church. If this spirituality stuff was real, I wanted to see or hear proof.

At that moment, I began to see visions. First, of bird feathers, where I was holding one in my hand and gently touching a person's forehead, and as I looked behind them, there were millions of people as far as the eye can see. I was scared of how big that vision was, yet somehow I knew that I was going to guide people on their healing journey.

I saw my friend Tony and my Aunt Jenny, who both died of cancer, and I saw how if I had known about plant medicine and energy earlier, maybe I could have done something to help them. I saw visions of so many beautiful people in the world who have no idea about energy and the power we all have to heal.

More and more visions and downloads came to me too fast to be processed or remembered.

I kept crying and shaking, and despite all the visions, all I could think about was the woman from Colombia and when I would find my real, true love. And so I cried out to God once more, "God, please, I am so tired of waiting. I am so tired of searching, please tell me, please show me. Who is the one for me?"

At that moment, something happened that changed my life forever. My right arm lifted toward the heavens, trembling and pointing up above. It wasn't me picking it up, my arm was literally acting on its own. Once it was fully extended and pointing straight up, it started to turn and point toward me until finally, it landed on my heart. My hand kept tapping my heart over and over again, and in that moment, I realized:

The one I've been looking for all my life was *me*.

As this happened, I heard God's voice speak to me: "*You*. You are the one. You are the one you've been searching for your entire life."

WHAT YOU SEEK LIES WITHIN

When we're quiet and still, we see that the answers to most of the questions we've been asking all along about our lives have always been within. Yet sometimes we put ourselves in situations that cause us to feel immense pain, because only through the suffering will we reach surrender and transcend the state of disconnection to our inner knowing. There comes a moment when the weight of not knowing (caused by separation) becomes too heavy to carry, and we finally stop fighting to hold on to it. And in that release, in surrendering, we re-open ourselves to truth. The truth of just how powerful we actually are. We finally feel free to dream again, and this time, to actually embody and live it. That's when we finally become free to create our dream life.

Yet we can only create our dream life if we allow ourselves to step into it, and that takes us back to our relationship with fear, courage, and real love. For me, I was afraid to say, "She's not the one," because I was so infatuated with the idea of being with a woman from Colombia, and I was scared not just to let her go, but to let go of the idea of her.

Yet that wasn't love.

Look closely, and you'll see that I was attached, and the energy under that attachment was fear. How was I ever going to open up to real love, or real life, if I had all of that desperate desire and fear stuck within? How would I open to love if I was constantly looking for the answers to my life, and looking for love, outside of myself? I couldn't. I wouldn't. It's literally impossible. That's how most people end up with a mind mate and not a soul mate.

Fear didn't want me to say, "She's not the one," because for that belief to die, something inside of me had to die with it. The part of me that was dependent on a woman to feel loved, and the attachment to finding "the one," had to die. How else could the version of me who saw himself as whole and complete, regardless of his relationship status, be born?

So I had to have the courage to let go of me, the only me I knew, the version of me who was in a perpetual state of asking, "Are you the one?"

I had to be willing to release who I was and the energy that had created this version of my life.

Until this moment, everything you have been creating has been from your old self, the one filled with negative stories, limiting beliefs, fears, worries, and doubts. Sometimes, you don't want to hear or speak the truth, because you don't know how to live in that truth. I didn't. And yet the truth truly is what set me free. It will for you too. Whether it's about a relationship, your health, career, or finances, there is something you have been seeking in the external world that can only be found internally, and you're being called to let go of whatever that is and the energy underneath it.

The journey in life is getting to this moment when you realize that everything you have ever wanted was always within reach. Because it was always within you.

You are the one.

Everything you have ever wanted was always within reach. Because it was always within you. Because you are the one.

You've been taught systematically, subtly, and from birth that the answers you seek about life, purpose, identity, and direction live outside of you. You've been taught to find them in podcasts, books, religion, teachers, social media, anywhere but in *you*. You've been taught to look outside of yourself for answers, for help, for saving because you've been conditioned that way.

When you finally realize on an energetic level that the answers you've been seeking have always been inside of you, then that means all that came before has to dissolve. Not in shame, but in gratitude, because without all of it, you would never have truly valued the gift of that inner voice the way you now do.

From this magical moment on, you can listen within and no longer outsource your truth. You can release the attachment to the limiting beliefs, dismantle the negative stories, and transcend the energy of separation that lives beneath them.

To realize all of this, I had to let go of the woman. I had to stop seeking "the one" outside of myself. Because as long as I was chasing completion in someone else, I'd always be abandoning the one place it could only ever truly be found, and that is within.

It's the same thing for you. Maybe it's not seeking a woman or man, but in some aspect of your life, you want answers from the outside. Maybe it's approval, permission, validation, a sign, but somewhere in your life you're still reaching and hoping that someone or something will finally give you permission to be who you already are.

This is my invitation to you to *stop.*

To release the attachment to anything external and to start feeling internally for what's right. To begin the slow, beautiful, and sacred journey of returning to your own inner compass. It's scary, because that voice is quieter than fear, but also truer.

Within each of us, there is a place inside where we feel and know that something is so right, it can't be wrong, and something is so wrong, it can't be right. Let this be your new guidance, and from that energy, may you start creating whatever you want, because when you reach this place, you have returned to your heart.

When you start this journey and choose to live from the power of what's within, instead of the dependency of what's out there, profound shifts will begin to take place. At first, it's subtle and quiet as you feel a pull to not speak or react but to instead listen and feel. Since love is a higher frequency, you'll also feel resistance from the old people-pleaser, dependent-on-external-validation part of you. It'll try to guilt you back into staying small, because it knows it will not survive in the light of who you're becoming.

And that's the beautiful paradox of it all. Again, the old must die for the new to be born.

The more you do this—listening to yourself, speaking your truth, and releasing the old attachments—the easier it becomes in the future. If you keep going through this process of death and rebirth, a process I've been through a thousand times, it's bumpy, yet I promise you, eventually, one day you'll wake up and realize there was never anything to fear in the first place.

You are becoming someone new, someone who has always been inside of you. Someone patiently waiting for you to realize, to remember the truth of it all—of how this reality works, of what you're capable of, and of who you actually are.

THIS IS YOUR RETURN

I don't believe the truth about who we are has ever been told in the way I'm about to share it, at least not from the heart. I want you to know that my love goes out to you if you're currently at a point in your journey where you believe someone outside of you is coming to save you, or that redemption lies in the hands of another. I know what you're feeling and believing, as it was a part of my journey too.

Yet if this book has softened your vision and opened your heart, even a little, and you're open to seeing with different eyes . . . I invite you to keep reading. If not, that's okay. You can skip to the conclusion and know all is well.

What I'm about to share isn't something I learned. It isn't something anyone taught me. It's something I experienced, gained access to, and now embody. It came through years of inner excavation. Of going deep within myself and facing my fears head on. It came through silence, through tears, through moments of release and surrender when I wanted nothing more than to control and hold on.

And more than anything, through moments of communion and receiving from the Divine, moments so profound that human words can't begin to describe them.

All of this is available to all of us. Available to you when you're ready. Available if this is your lifetime to experience it.

There are many examples of what this looks like, this kind of journey, connection, and knowing. One of the clearest is Jesus. He wasn't the exception to humanity . . . he was the example of it. He came to show us what's possible when a soul surrenders all illusion of separation and releases all barriers, mental, emotional, spiritual, and physical. He showed us what's possible when we transcend separation and speak from union with Source.

Jesus didn't arrive to be worshipped. When you're one with all, there is no looking up or down. He came to unlock the ability for union with the Divine for us all. And he isn't the only one to walk this path. He is one luminous thread in a beautiful tapestry of beings across cultures and times who have realized and are starting to realize their divinity. Not as a hierarchy over others, but as a return to wholeness within. From Buddha, to Mary Magdalene, to Paramahansa Yogananda, and more recently Ram Dass. This truth and this potential keep showing up in different vessels when they are ready to access and carry it.

And now the invitation is for it to show up in you.

This moment, if you allow it, is the activation of your own remembrance. Not a memory from your mind, but one stored deep within your bones, in your breath, and in the stillness beneath every thought.

You see, the kingdom of heaven is not coming from the sky. It isn't after death. It isn't earned, bartered, or bestowed.

It's here. It's within. It's YOU.

Heaven isn't a location, it's a frequency, a vibration, and a lens. And the only requirement to enter? That's your willingness to forgive, to let go, and to choose love. Again, and again.

The human journey is the soul's choice to forget just enough to one day be able to remember again. That remembrance happens when you turn inward, choose healing over hiding, truth over fear, wholeness over division.

The truth is you aren't separate from God . . . you never were. And you don't need anything or anyone else to validate your access to that truth.

That is the real teaching, the real invitation. Not to bow at the feet of an awakened soul, but to rise and expand into the light of your own. And with every moment of healing, letting go and choosing love instead of fear, you rise just a bit further, until one day you remember fully and become what you've always been: whole, worthy, divine . . . you.

You are the one. You are it all, you are everything you've been seeking, you are magnificent and beautiful, and you've been it all . . . since the moment you were born.

AWAKEN YOU
Oneness Declaration

Close your eyes, sit in silence, take three slow breaths, and place your hand over your heart, declaring out loud: "I'm ready to Awaken. I'm ready to remember. I'm ready to live in union with all there is, all of life, and all that I am."

This is your return. The end of the story you were told, and the beginning of the truth you've always been.

CONCLUSION

Welcome Home

I remember when I first went to an Evangelical church, and I saw people in the pews speaking in tongues. I had no idea what I was seeing, so after the service, I asked people what had happened to them.

"I heard God," one person said.

"God spoke to me," another shared in awe.

"What did 'He' say?" I asked in wonder.

"God told me . . ." and they shared with me the most miraculous things. God talked to them about their relationships, health, children, jobs . . . everything. It sounded so cool that I wanted to be just like those people. I wanted God to speak to me too, to tell me about life, relationships, love, you name it.

And so every Sunday, I'd go to church and pray, "Please, speak to me, God. Please let me hear your voice."

I never heard anything, and I'd think, *I need to pray harder.* So the next Sunday would come, and I prayed even harder, only to still hear silence. Sunday after Sunday passed, and I never heard God's voice. My prayers soon turned to pleas and promises, yet I was only met by stillness.

Flash forward almost 20 years later to the first time I ever took ayahuasca. There I was with the medicine inside of me, working its way through me, when I felt a sudden urge to lie on the ground, so I did. I felt both my hands rise to settle upon my chest. I laid there in stillness for what felt like hours, but it was probably only minutes, then I felt one arm start twitching, and the other began flapping like a wing in the wind.

And that was when I heard a voice speak to me in Spanish, saying words that roughly translate to "I'm about to transform your life in the same way that a caterpillar transforms into a butterfly."

The next thing I saw was a cocoon, and as it opened, I saw myself fly out of it. In that moment, I realized: I was on a journey of transformation. I intentionally chose the butterfly as my company's logo, because my journey was, and still is, one of transformation.

What you have started with this book is a lot like the butterfly's journey. Like me, like the butterfly, you are undergoing a metamorphosis, changing from one form, one person, into another.

The beauty of this work is it doesn't end with you. As your vibration rises, it becomes a blueprint and permission slip for those around you. It will touch the lives of the seven people closest to you. And from them, it continues rippling out.

This is a process that never ends. Even today, after all my inner work, I'm still awakening, healing, and transforming. You will too, if you choose to continue on this journey. Yes, sometimes it's hard. Sometimes pain comes with it, and sometimes you'll face people, circumstances, events, thoughts, and emotions that shake you to your soul.

Yet with each step you take, you are one step closer to returning home.

Home to your heart.

Home to oneness with all.

And home to your highest self.

RESOURCES

Take a moment for yourself.

Your life is calling you into a deeper level of clarity and you do not have to guess what your next step should be. I created a short quiz that gives you personalized results based on where you truly are in your emotional and spiritual journey.

These results will show you the specific guidance, practices, and support that match what you need right now. Many people are surprised by how accurate and revealing their results are because it reflects what they have been feeling but have not fully put into words. It takes less than two minutes and the direction you receive can shift the way you move forward from here.

Scan the QR code. Discover what life is asking you to step into next.

ENDNOTES

1. Brené Brown, "Shame vs. Guilt," Brené Brown, LLC, January 15, 2013, https://brenebrown.com/articles/2013/01/15/shame-v-guilt/.

2. David G. Pearson and Tony Craig, "The Great Outdoors? Exploring the Mental Health Benefits of Natural Environments," *Frontiers in Psychology* 5 (October 21, 2014): 1178. https://pmc.ncbi.nlm.nih.gov/articles/PMC4204431/.

3. Marcia P. Jimenez et al., "Associations Between Nature Exposure and Health: A Review of the Evidence," *International Journal of Environmental Research and Public Health* 18, no. 9 (April 30, 2021): 4790. https://pmc.ncbi.nlm.nih.gov/articles/PMC8125471/.

ACKNOWLEDGMENTS

For years, I knew I was going to write this book. I saw it and felt it so strongly. I just didn't know *when* it would come through. Now that it has, I can see how perfectly timed—like everything in life—it is.

Like most authors say, "it takes a village" to create a book, and this one was no different.

Let me start with our incredible team at Morel Global, who passionately believe in our mission to awaken, heal, and transform lives. It's a true honor and privilege to work beside you every day, to see and feel your energy at our live events and our weekly calls. Your effort, commitment, and energy inspire me to keep forging ahead, so thank you.

To Reid Tracy, Patty Gift, Anne Barthel, and the entire Hay House team who have helped make this book possible. Thank you for believing in me, in my message, and in my mission. Choosing to work with you as publisher was such an easy decision for me. I'm honored to join the Hay House family and to be a part of your mission, purpose, and energy too.

To Amanda Ibey, I don't even know where to start. Without you, I literally couldn't have done this book! Thank you for being an amazing collaborator and writing partner with me, and for your honesty, patience, and skill in helping me to share and shape this story. I'm grateful for you.

To Jaidree Braddix, you are *the* best agent in the world. You believed in me and this book long before anyone else. You helped me polish the proposal, find the perfect publisher and collaborator, and have had my back every step of the way right until the end. Thank you for all you've done for me and this book.

To Mother Aya and all the medicines in life that have helped me to heal the hidden wounds and to see with my heart.

I could never have written this book without my family. To my kids, Isaiah, Micah, Aaron, and Selena, thank you for your love, patience, and for "sharing me" with this book as I spent mornings, nights, weekends, and vacation time furiously typing away on my keyboard. At the heart of everything I do are all of you. You inspire me to become the man and father I'm working to become. You help give me purpose, and I'm proud of each and every one of you. I love you!

To Jen, what I feel for you and our connection goes beyond words. Thank you for showing me what unconditional love is, and for having the courage to work on yourself, so you can find your inner light. Your commitment to yourself gives me the space and inspires me to continue working on myself. Without you, your love, and your light, this book wouldn't have been possible. I love you!

A special thanks to Andy and Jo, thank you for accepting me, believing in me, and loving me from the start. I am grateful to you both.

I know I wrote a lot about my parents and childhood, and the hidden wounds that I received. You never know how messages will actually resonate with someone, so while I can't fully control how the stories will land with readers, I sincerely hope that I never came across as resenting or angry at my parents. It's truly the opposite.

To my dad, thank you for giving me life, for reconnecting with me, and for teaching me the most beautiful and powerful lesson we can learn: forgiveness and acceptance.

Finally, to my mom. How can I express the depth of love, connection, and gratitude that I feel? I can't. Words can't do it justice. Not only did she give me life, but she showed me what this life is truly all about and pointed the way for me to follow.

ABOUT THE AUTHOR

DANNY MOREL is a spiritual teacher, speaker, and global thought leader in human awakening who has helped millions achieve abundance in their finances, relationships, and health through deep healing work and spiritual awakenings. He's the founder of Awaken Your Highest Self, one of the fastest-growing spiritual events in the world. He also hosts *The Higher Self* podcast, which has billions of downloads and hit the #1 spot in its category within six months of launch. Danny offers private coaching, retreats, and masterclasses. He is also a recognized thought leader who is frequently featured in major national media such as *Forbes*, *Entrepreneur*, and *Business Insider*.

www.dannymorel.com

Hay House Titles of Related Interest

YOU CAN HEAL YOUR LIFE, the movie,
starring Louise Hay & Friends
(available as an online streaming video)
www.hayhouse.com/louise-movie

THE SHIFT, the movie,
starring Dr. Wayne W. Dyer
(available as an online streaming video)
Learn more at www.hayhouse.com/the-shift-movie

***

BECOMING SUPERNATURAL: How Common People Are Doing the Uncommon, by Dr. Joe Dispenza

THE GREATNESS MINDSET: Unlock the Power of Your Mind and Live Your Best Life Today, by Lewis Howes

PURE HUMAN: The Hidden Truth of Our Divinity, Power, and Destiny, by Gregg Braden

SELF HELP: This Is Your Chance to Change Your Life, by Gabrielle Bernstein

All of the above are available at your local bookstore, or may be ordered by contacting Hay House (see next page).

***

We hope you enjoyed this Hay House book. If you'd like to receive our online catalog featuring additional information on Hay House books and products, or if you'd like to find out more about the Hay Foundation, please contact:

Hay House LLC, P.O. Box 5100, Carlsbad, CA 92018-5100
(760) 431-7695 or (800) 654-5126
www.hayhouse.com® • www.hayfoundation.org

Published in Australia by:
Hay House Australia Publishing Pty Ltd
18/36 Ralph St., Alexandria NSW 2015
Phone: +61 (02) 9669 4299
www.hayhouse.com.au

Published in the United Kingdom by:
Hay House UK Ltd
1st Floor, Crawford Corner,
91–93 Baker Street, London W1U 6QQ
Phone: +44 (0)20 3927 7290
www.hayhouse.co.uk

Published in India by:
Hay House Publishers (India) Pvt Ltd
Muskaan Complex, Plot No. 3,
B-2, Vasant Kunj, New Delhi 110 070
Phone: +91 11 41761620
www.hayhouse.co.in